SCULPTING DOLLS IN SUPER SCULPEY®

By Cheryl Riello

Jones Publishing, Inc.

SCULPTING DOLLS IN SUPER SCULPEY®
By Cheryl Riello

Publisher
Gregory Bayer

Editor
Kim Shields

Production Team
Jean Adams
Cindy Boutwell
Bruce Loppnow
Cindy McCarville

Cover Design
Rebecca Haas

Cover Photos
Mary Kay Berg

Published By:
Jones Publishing, Inc.
N7450 Aanstad Road
P.O. Box 5000
Iola, WI 54945
Phone: (715) 445-5000
Fax: (715) 445-4053

This book is available at special discounts for bulk purchases. For prices or other information contact the publisher at the above address.

10 9 8 7 6 5 4 3 2 1

Printed in the United States

ISBN 1-879825-20-1

About the Author

Cheryl Riello has been studying art for over 20 years. She has studied at the Creative Arts Workshop and the John Slade Ely House in New Haven, Connecticut. She has attended many workshops, seminars and classes experimenting with different mediums of art, including painting, drawing, pottery, jewelry making and soft-sculpture.

Ms. Riello's study of three-dimensional visual art, combined with her interest in using different materials for sculpting, has led to her creation of an incredibly "lifelike" collection of hand-sculpted people. These dolls are crafted from a combination of one or more materials, including Super Sculpey, Polyform, Cernit, Fimo and Paperclay. All of the dressings are hand-sewn and elaborately detailed. Ms. Riello uses antique fabrics and trimmings as often as possible.

A feature article on Ms. Riello's sculptures appeared in the Yale University newspaper, **"Yale Weekly Bulletin and Calendar"**, in May of 1988. She has featured her sculptures in several galleries in New Haven and surrounding areas. In 1988, she featured over 100 of her sculptures in a solo exhibit at the Wave Gallery Annex, located in the Shubert Performing Arts Center Complex in New Haven. That year she was also a featured artist in the "Fun and Fantasy for the Holidays" show at the same gallery.

Ms. Riello is a sociologist and has a degree in business. She is a member of the International Dollmakers Association and the Connecticut Guild of Doll Crafters. She is also an active member of the Arts Council of Greater New Haven. Ms. Riello recently became the Regional Captain of the International Artists Support Group, based in Washington, DC.

From 1992 to 1994, Ms. Riello's creations were sold exclusively at Paddywhack's Attic, a collector's doll shop in Essex, Connecticut. Currently, Ms. Riello is selling her dolls through mail order. Ms. Riello's dolls are featured in the "Fresh Faces" section of the November, 1993 issue of Dolls, The Collector's Magazine, and again another doll is featured in the "Fresh Faces" section of the February, 1994 issue of Dolls, The Collector's Magazine. A full color page of Ms. Riello's dolls are featured in the "Gallery" section of the March, 1994 issue of the most popular doll magazine in the United States, Contemporary Doll Magazine. The Aug/Sept 1994 issue of Contemporary Doll Collector magazine features Ms. Riello's dolls, "Mr. Yubin and Grandpa Tyler" in the Debut Section.

A "how to" article written by Ms. Riello appeared in the Sept/Oct 1994 issue of Dollmaking: Projects and Plans. This article described how to make a customized clown. There is a biographical article about Ms. Riello (titled "One Artist's Evolution") and a photograph in the on-line library of the Crafts Forum of CompuServe. The Victorian Mercantile will feature an article and photograph of Ms. Riello's work in the magazine scheduled for release in early 1995. The Dec/Jan issue of Contemporary Doll Collector features one of Ms. Riello's cats called "Chenille."

Ms. Riello will have several projects published in upcoming Dollmaking: Projects and Plans magazine in the coming year. ■

Please Read This!

This book was produced for the entertainment and enlightenment of dollmakers. While every effort has been made to ensure that the information contained herein is correct and up-to-date, the editor, author, and publisher extend no warranty as to the accuracy or completeness of the information—there may be mistakes, both typographical and in content. Therefore, this text should be used only as a general guide and not as the ultimate source of information.

This book is sold with the understanding that the publisher is not engaged in rendering product endorsements or providing instruction as a substitute for appropriate training by qualified sources. Therefore, Jones Publishing, Inc. and the author, Cheryl Riello, shall have neither liability nor responsibility to any person or entity with respect to any loss or damage caused, or alleged to be caused, directly or indirectly, by the information contained in this book.

We hope you enjoy reading *Sculpting Dolls in Super Sculpey*®.

Table of Contents

Dedication

This book is dedicated with love to my best friend,
my husband, Christopher.

Introduction

Dollmaking is an art that has evolved around the world throughout the centuries. As technology advances more rapidly every day, original dollmaking has grown to become of great interest to hobbyists and doll enthusiasts. Today, although there is great demand for popular, mass-produced dolls, there are many collectors who want a one-of-a kind piece by a lesser known artist. Whether you are interested in dollmaking as a hobby or a career, pursuing it will be rewarding. It is the ultimate form of expression. When you make a doll, you have control over every part of the creative process from the beginning to the end. You not only sculpt the face, limbs, and body, but you are also the fashion designer, the hairstylist, the make-up artist, the jeweler, the shoe-maker and much more. The limitations are defined by you. Helen Bullard in *The American Doll Artist* Volume I, said, "Even the most primitive artist or craftsman works with what he knows from his experience; often the very limitation assures a more direct and revealing expression."

In dollmaking, like any hobby, there are numerous avenues to explore. The best way to start is to buy dollmaking magazines and decide which type of doll appeals to you. Dollmakers should become familiar with other dollmakers and their work. Some magazines specialize in porcelain dollmaking, others are for dollmakers in general, and still others are for doll collectors. When you choose to make a particular type of doll, you may want to subscribe to a few magazines. Most of the doll magazines include calendars of doll shows throughout the United States. You can usually find one in your area that will introduce you to a variety of dolls, dollmakers, doll and doll supply dealers, doll collectors, and doll enthusiasts.

Dollmaking has become a part of my life. For me, it is a form of relaxation. It is quality time that I have for myself and it is also good therapy. When I am intently working on a project, I am completely absorbed into another world. I can escape to this world and find comfort.

Making dolls fits in very well with a busy lifestyle. With even a few minutes of spare time, I can pick up something and work on it. Oven baked clays are especially good because you can turn on your oven and cure one piece at a time.

The purpose of this book is to provide the beginning and the experienced dollmaker with a source that covers the basic techniques of original dollmaking. It takes you through these steps and explains the reasons for doing them. It is a guide to help you create your own unique, one-of a-kind dolls. By learning the basics, you can go on to create your own works of art. I have kept the techniques and patterns simple, so as you practice, you can elaborate on what you have learned.

The first project is a clown because I think it is the easiest type of doll to make. The facial features are simple lines, such as a ball for a nose. By keeping the face simple, it is certain that you will be happy with the results. Painting an expression on the face helps to soften any awkward sculpting which can be a blessing for the first time dollmaker. The body is a very simple, basic pattern—it is unisex and perhaps a bit oversized. The costume is also simple, it leaves plenty of room for gathering at the neck, wrists and ankles. The hands are plain and the shoes are not clearly defined. Thus, keeping them to scale is not as important as with the other dolls.

The second project, Grandma, touches upon some more detailed features: placement of glass eyes, wrinkles, and crevices in the face. The project explores sculpting fingernails, and the placement of eyelashes and eyebrows. Also introduced is fitting the costume and making accessories such as glasses and a cane. You will need to concentrate more on the scale for this doll.

The Floozy, which is the third project, is fun. It elaborates on features like long eyelashes and fingernails. She wears a lot of bright make-up and ornate jewelry. You will learn to make a breast plate and costume her to reveal it. Feet and toes will be sculpted and the doll will be able to stand freely in high heel open-toe sandals.

The fourth project, a child, includes a change of scale. This is good practice in learning to create any age doll you wish. The way the doll is constructed and sculpted is the same as it is for adult dolls, but the difference is in the size—everything will be done on a smaller scale. ■

Tools & Supplies

There are a variety of tools and supplies that can be used to sculpt your dolls. I have grouped them into three categories; sculpting tools, household tools and miscellaneous supplies. The sculpting tools are simple and basic and are sold in art supply stores. I also like to experiment with different utensils I find around the house. Be creative and keep your mind and eyes open to everyday objects that can be used when making your dolls. Miscellaneous supplies are just that, miscellaneous. They are all easy to find and are frequently used.

Sculpting Tools
- Blunt-edged tool like a nutpick or round-edged toothpick. It smooths small details. It also does the initial blending of larger pieces (for example, blending the neck to the head) before your fingers can take over and finish. It punctures holes and draws thick lines. If the other end is rounded, it helps to make eye sockets and round indentations (shown second from right in photo).
- Sharp-edged tool for finer detail work such as the nostrils, ear holes, fingers, etc. (shown at far right in photo). A hat pin works well. A toothpick also works well in some situations. I have found similar tools in the minia ture tool kits that are sold in hardware or grocery stores.
- X-acto® knife for drawing sharp, clean lines and cutting the clay and other thin materials (shown third from left in photo).

Household Supplies
- Aluminum foil for the base of the head.
- Broiler pan for curing the clay.
- Hot glue gun to adhere mohair to the Super Sculpey head. It is also useful for securing accessories like bows, flowers and feathers such as for the Clown's hat.
- Large piece of tile surface for working with clay and sculpting (shown in photo). It is portable, flat and easy to keep clean.
- Masking tape to wrap the armature.
- Rolling pin to roll clay out flat.
- Small manicuring scissors for trimming eyelashes and eyebrows.
- Tweezers for selecting strands of mohair or sheep's wool for the doll's hair.
- Wax paper or tracing paper for pattern making.

Miscellaneous Supplies
- Acrylic paints for painting various parts of the doll.
- Clear-drying glue.
- Fine paint brush for detail work and a fuller brush is needed for larger areas.
- Floral wire to secure the muslin arms and legs to the clay bodies.
- Jewelry glue.
- Matte and gloss finishes are needed for the final coat.
- Muslin for the doll body.
- Pliers to secure the wire together (shown second from left in photo). Working with a small pair of pliers is less cumbersome.
- Polyester batting for stuffing the doll.
- Quilt batting to fill out the torso before stuffing.
- Small ruler for accurate measuring (shown at far left in photo).
- Steel wire—14 or 16 gauge. I prefer 14 gauge; it is harder to bend but the extra strength will enable the doll to stand alone along with protecting the wire from snapping when bending and straightening it.
- Toothpick to apply strands of hair with glue.
- Wire cutter that will cut 14 or 16 gauge wire.

Clay

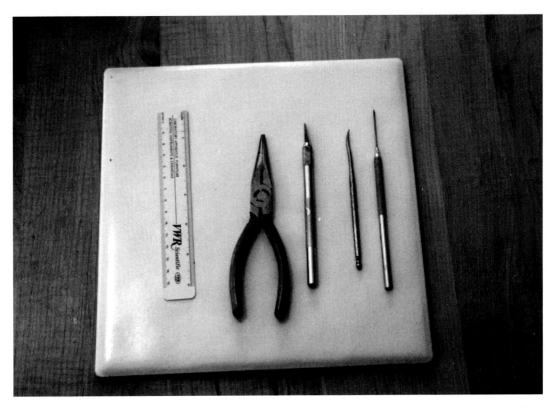

Above (from left to right): ruler, pliers, X-acto® knife, blunt-edged tool, sharp-edged tool.
A tile square is underneath the tools.

Clay

I used Super Sculpey® for the four projects in this book. There are many different types of oven-baked clays on the market. You can experiment with a variety to see which ones you find easiest to use and which ones finish the way you like best. I buy Super Sculpey® in bulk from the Polyform Products Company in Illinois. Directions about storage and curing are on the box. If you are interested in purchasing a smaller amount of clay, there are numerous stores and shops which advertise mail orders in the back of most doll magazines.

Unlike a lot of clays I have tried, Super Sculpey® is extremely versatile. It is pliable enough to be worked over and over and it doesn't get soft or lose shape from the warmth of your hands. It does not shrink when cured, and when dried, the surface can be easily accessorized with paint, cosmetics, and glue. When painting, I use a finish over the paint to prevent chipping. It can be a gloss, matte, or wax finish. I have also found cosmetics, such as blush, stay on Super Sculpey® very well. I have some dolls that are 15 years old and the blush is still on their cheeks. For painting lips and fingernails, nail polish can be used and it will adhere rather well. While a hot glue gun works well for adhering mohair to the Super Sculpey® head, when two pieces of clay break and need to be joined together, the only thing I have found to work well is epoxy glue. If you are looking for a wax-like effect, any floor wax will do just fine. It gives a nice finish over painted or bare clay. There are also several waxes especially made for dollmaking. These can be found in most doll supply catalogues. Drying the piece outside cuts down on the smell and dries the clay thoroughly.

As with anything new, it is a good idea to practice and experiment with the clay. Take out a piece, roll it and shape it and try making a head with it. Then, roll it up and do something else. You have to be willing to use trial and error. The cliché—practice make perfect—has never been more appropriate.

Handling

Handling & Storage of Clay

Clay can get dirty and pick up lint and other particles from handling. I always work from a one pound slab that is stored in a plastic bag with a resealable top. From that one pound plastic bag, I separate out two or three strips at a time and store those pieces in another resealable bag. Always wash your hands before using. If you have to leave a piece while sculpting, wrap it in a clean paper towel and put it in a plastic bag. Once the clay is dirty or discolored, it will bake in and you will not be able to leave it with a bare finish. I keep another bag for pieces of clay that are dirty and I use them for legs or shoes if there are going to be covered up with stockings and shoes.

According to the directions, since Super Sculpey® stays dry indefinitely until baking, it should be stored in a cool place.

Curing

The best way to get familiar with the curing process is to experiment. Shape a head, a pair of hands or feet, and then cure them. Read the Super Sculpey® directions carefully before baking. If you make a mistake, be ready to throw the piece out and practice on another. Remember, this clay is for practice only. To cure the pieces of clay:

1. Cover a small baking pan with foil and place the pieces on this to bake.
2. Set the oven to 275 degrees. Place the pieces in the oven. You do not have to preheat the oven first. If using acrylic or plastic eyes, place the head in a cold oven. I have been told by several doll eye manu facturing companies that the piece should heat up with the oven so the eyes get used to the rise in tem perature and don't melt. If you are using glass eyes, it doesn't matter whether you preheat the oven or not as they are temperature resistant.
3. Time your pieces. The directions on the Super Sculpey box say to bake the clay for 15-20 minutes. For thinner pieces such as arms, etc. I like to check the piece after 10 minutes and every 10 minutes there after. For thicker pieces, you can start checking after 15 minutes.
4. The way to tell if a piece is ready may be difficult to the unexperienced eye. The color will darken slight ly. When it first comes out of the oven, it will be a little soft. A minute later it will start to harden. It will continue to darken a bit more as it cools. Bake the clay thoroughly because it will break very easily if not cured well. You can tell if you over bake the clay for the fumes will be obnoxious. The clay will become brittle and will turn a dark color. You may see white markings inside.
5. Always ventilate! Open a window while the clay is baking.
6. Cool the pieces on a cool rack or a trivet. If the pieces are attached by wire, don't touch the wire. Even though the clay cools quickly, the wire remains hot. You may need potholders to take it off the pan.

Scale

Before you can successfully make a doll, you must understand proportion. Generally, an adult doll should measure 7-1/2 to 8 heads tall. A child will measure about half of that, maybe less depending on their age. To study the proportions of the human body, I recommend reading the *Atlas of Human Anatomy for the Artist* by Stephen Rogers Peck. This book covers scale and body parts. If you are having trouble sculpting an ear or if you cannot find the right body proportion for a doll, this book will help.

The size of your doll's head will determine the height of your doll. When you have finished sculpting and curing your doll's head, measure from the top of the head to the chin. Use a piece of graph paper either 8-1/2 x 11 inches or 8-1/2 by 14 inches to sketch out your doll. Take those measurements and draw 8 heads down the graph paper (see *Sketch of Adult Figure*). For example, my doll's head measured 2 inches in length and 2 inches in width. (Please note that the figure sketches at the right are shown at 50%.) I drew 8 heads down the graph paper, 2 inches wide. This doll should stand about 16 inches tall. Once you have drawn these heads down the page, use the following guides as a basis for shaping the proportions of the figure.

Figure Sketches

Adult Figure Sketch

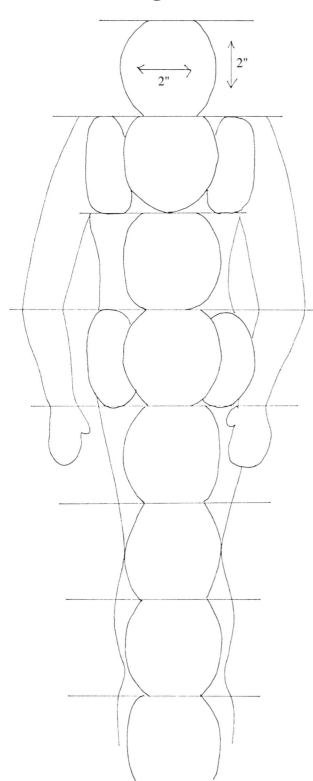

Figure sketches are shown at 50% of actual size. The measurements (2" and 1-1/4") are the measurements at 100%.

Child Figure Sketch

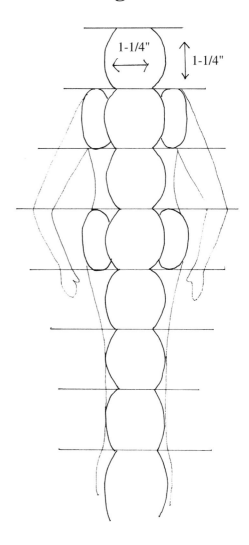

Figure sketches shown at 50%

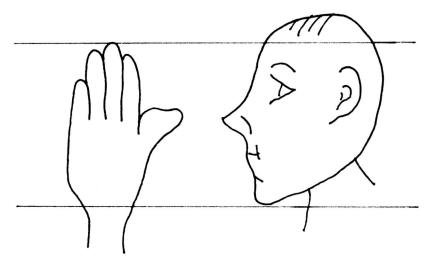

Hand Measurement

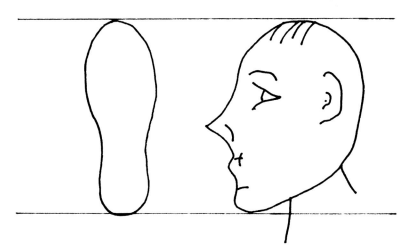

Foot Measurement

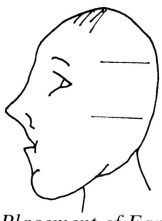

Placement of Ear

Scale & Sculpting

Scale (continued)

Generally, for an adult doll, the measurement from the top of the head to the waist is 3 heads. The hip is equal to 1-1/2 heads. The legs are 3-1/2 to 4 heads in length. The elbow is on the same level as the waist line. The head reaches one-half of the way from the hip to the knee. On a female, the width of the hip is the same as the shoulder width (usually 3 heads from side to side).

Children are generally about half the size of adults. Follow the same units of measurement as for the adult doll (see *Child Figure Sketch*). The length of my child's head measures about 1-1/4 inches in height and in width. The finished doll should be 8-9 inches tall. Draw 8 heads (the size of the child's head) down a page of graph paper and divide the body as done for the adult doll.

Once you have finished your sketched figure, the following measurements will help in determining the size of the hands and feet. Again, using the head as a unit of measurement, a foot equals the measurement from the chin to the top of the head (see *Foot Measurement Sketch*). A hand, measured from the wrist to the top of the middle finger, measures from the middle of the hairline to the chin (see *Hand Measurement Sketch*).

There are many variations, especially when making character dolls. For example, on a clown, the feet will be exaggerated. Some characters have shorter waists, longer necks and legs, etc. Elderly people are generally shorter. You may want to start the head at about 6 inches tall or scrunch up the body as I have done with my "Grandma.." There is nothing wrong with slight variations, but it must look right to the eye.

Sculpting

Sculpting is an art that takes a lot of practice and experimentation. Nothing is achieved in a day, a week or even a month. It can take as long as six months to a year to really like something you have sculpted, but it will happen, you just have to keep practicing until you do it right.

Sometimes the best thing to do after you have sculpted something over and over is to put it down for a while and come back with a fresh mind. And, after sculpting some good pieces, you may find that your work regresses some. Don't worry, your next project will be better!

It is a good idea to do some research before you begin. Either go to the library or purchase some books on the subjects you are interested in. Some of the books I have purchased have become my most valuable resources through the years. *Modeling the Head in Clay Sculpture* by Bruno Lucchesi and Margit Malmstrom, and *Modeling a Likeness in Clay* by Grubbs, are two books which are very helpful for all experience levels, including beginners. The first, *Modeling the Head in Clay*, takes you step by step through the process of modeling a bust of a person. The photographs in this book are large and they show the process of sculpting features in detail. The second, *Modeling a Likeness in Clay* is done exactly the same way as *Modeling the Head in Clay* only it takes you step by step through the sculpting of an elderly person, a woman, a child, and describes ethnic features on other people. It also explains scale as well.

The *Artist's Complete Guide to Facial Expressions* by Gary Faigin, is a good resource if you need ideas for your doll's facial features. The book illustrates many different facial poses and how each one effects the total facial expression.

Some basic points of sculpting are:

1. Always keep to the scale of the project you are working on. Keep the eyes, ears, nose, mouth, etc. in scale with the head. Some features can be exaggerated, but only to a slight degree before the piece becomes distorted.
2. Always keep the head, hands and feet in proportion. Some exceptions apply, like clown shoes.
3. When starting to sculpt the face, follow the diagram for the vertical and horizontal line placement of the features.
4. Use clean fingers to smooth the clay when working on larger areas. Work with small pieces of clay and

keep alternating building the piece up by adding clay and then smoothing either with the blunt tool or your fingers. Repeat this technique until you have reached the desired effect.

5. Symmetry is the key word when sculpting. Always do to one side what you do to the other. Turn the piece around and look at it from all angles. Go back and add or take off excess clay.

6. Always have a mirror handy and keep looking at yourself. You are the best model you have. Study other people as well. Magazines and catalogues sometimes have good close-ups of adults, children, and babies. Baby clothes catalogues have great photos of baby faces, hands, and feet. These publications also give you ideas about poses and fashion.

7. When working on the hands, look at your own for the size of each finger and the placement of the thumb. Do the same for the feet and toes. If you get the placement and size correct, the rest will come with practice.

8. Signing dolls. I sign my dolls on the palm of their hands. You may also do this on the soles of the feet or the back of the head. It doesn't matter. The main thing is that you sign your doll. Using a sharp tool, I carve my initials in the palm, with an abbreviated date and a small copyright symbol.

9. Sculpting the shoes allows the dolls to stand freely. If the soles of the feet are flat and the legs and shoes are sturdy enough to hold the weight of the doll, it will stand alone. Clay shoes can always be costumed to look like real shoes. Once you have made the shoe, you can glue material, felt, or leather to the uppers and it will be very difficult to see that the base is made of clay.

10. Be creative. As long as the proportions are right, the rest is up to the artist. There are no right or wrongs in any form of art. What you like and create will not please everyone because everyone's tastes are different. Pleasing yourself and achieving your personal goals are what is important.

Pattern-Making

Making patterns can be difficult and may seem confusing. In this book the patterns are basic and simple. While ready made patterns are included, how to make an original pattern to fit your doll is also explained. Always check the patterns in this book with your own doll. (Please note that some of the patterns have been reduced.) Since all of the dolls in this book are one-of-a-kind, it is impossible to judge how big or small your doll will come out. If your finished doll is larger in size and weight than the pattern shows, adjust the pattern on the doll and measure with a ruler or measuring tape how much extra material you will need for the width and length. Put the original pattern on graph paper and using it as a guide, add the extra amount. Reduce the pattern if the doll is smaller. Cut the new pattern out and mark it. Save the original pattern in case you want to make another doll of that size.

Use muslin for the body pattern. If the pattern looks too large, you may want to trim it after you cut it out on material. That way you can put the material against the doll and alter from there. When you come to the step that uses a ruler to alter the muslin arm and leg pattern by marking at the wrist, etc., keep in mind that the closer you trim the muslin to the limbs, the less you will have to alter after you sew. In other words, you may be able to eliminate the overlapping of muslin around the clay ridge before you glue it with wire. This will eliminate having to go back and sew the extra material to taper the doll.

Wax paper works well when you initially measure the doll because it is transparent and shows marks easily. You can even trace around the doll with your fingernails on the wax paper. You may want to transfer the wax paper pattern to graph paper or cardboard. If the pattern is going to be used often, i suggest using cardboard for it will hold up better.

The pattern pieces in this book can serve as a starting point for making more complicated costumes. An A-line dress can be embellished by added darts and gathering at the waist. Blouses can be easily transformed into blazers or coats by enlarging them and working in a heavier material.

I have included the clown's hat brim pattern and some of the cardboard shoe patterns. They can give you an idea about size. While you may not be able to follow them exactly because the size of your doll may differ slightly from mine, they will still be good guides if having to make your own pattern.

Costuming & Etc.

Costuming

When deciding how to costume your doll, be sure to think about scale. Do not use prints, plaids, stripes, etc. that are too large. Many fabric manufacturer's make "mini" patterned material. Some calicos are small enough and will do fine.

Keep in mind the weight of the material. Since the doll clothes are made on a small scale, heavier weights will be harder to work with and may seem bulky on the doll. Light, flowing, silky materials work well with evening dresses. Stiffer cottons make great children's jumpers and elderly ladies' housedresses. I usually wash the material first because it loosens up and falls better on the doll. If the material you are using is wrinkled, iron it before you start your project.

If you are looking for dramatic costuming, the library is a great place to get some ideas. A larger library will have a Leisure Section with illustrated books about different eras. Life Books publishes some great books such as *Life Goes to the Movies*, and *The Best of Life*. If you are looking for a book of period costumes, *The Historical Encyclopedia of Costumes*, by Albert Racinet, is a great resource of period costumes in other countries as well as in America.

Accessories

There are many craft stores and catalogues that carry accessories for dolls. If you are looking for props, check the measurements so that they are in scale with the size of the doll you are making. Doll magazines are a great source for any kind of doll supplies. Most doll supply companies will send a catalogue for little or no charge.

You may need to purchase various supplies not found locally from mail order companies. It is always wise to purchase a small amount of a product from a company you are not familiar with rather than a large order. For example, some mohair is better than others and will be easier to work with. Since the mohair is dyed, you may want to call the company and request a color chart showing small swatches of the colors they carry. Or, you can start with a sampling of a few colors like brown and gold. I prefer to work with wavy mohair. Straight mohair has no bend and doesn't fall well around the doll's face and body. Sheep wool is coarser and thicker than mohair and it comes in neutral colors like gray, brown and white. This wool makes very good wigs for elderly dolls because it keeps its shape. It can be found in some knitting shops and certain catalogues. If you are satisfied with the texture and color, order black, red, white and/or gray. All of the doll suppliers also carry wigs. You may prefer to use doll wigs and glue them on the doll's head rather than styling the mohair or sheep wool.

Follow the same procedure for ordering doll's eyes. Some companies send samples of one eye for color. Most companies have color charts or brochures which will help you in deciding what type and color. There are different eye shapes which are interesting and used for various purposes. You may want to start with a few different sizes and colors. For instance, 6mm, 8mm, 10mm and 12mm sizes are generally what you will be using. Purchasing 6mm, 8mm, and 10mm eyes in green, blue and brown will give you a variety of colors and sizes to work with. Once you are happy with a product, it is useful to have a small inventory of sizes and colors. This helps to reduce shipping costs and delays in delivery.

Jewelry

I collect costume jewelry to use for my dolls. I never throw out old jewelry that has broken and I ask all of my friends to remember me when they are cleaning out their jewelry boxes. Bits and pieces of broken jewelry work very well. You can also get jewelry from tag sales and flea markets. I keep costume jewelry findings in old spice jars and plastic organizers. I save clasps and thin chain, small charms, earrings, beads and just about anything that can be cut or shaped into tiny jewelry. Craft stores sell tiny rhinestones, pearls and a variety of accessories which allows you to create splendid pieces for your dolls.

Clown

This project, the clown, is the simplest of the four in this book. It will introduce you to the techniques of dollmaking without a lot of detail work. Many of the steps you'll learn in this project will be continued throughout the other three projects.

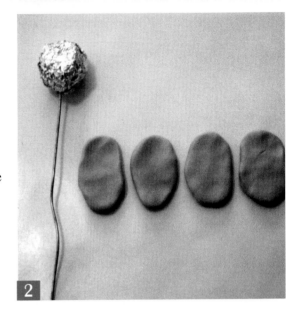

Beginning the Body

1. Cut six strands of wire about 10 inches long. These will be used for the legs, arms, head and torso. Cut two strands of wire about 12 inches long for the torso armature.

Beginning the Head

2. Make a small ball out of foil and run a 10 inch strand of wire through it. Extend a little of the wire over the top of the foil. With pliers, bend the top of the wire to make a hook and push it back down into the foil to bury and secure it.

3. On the side of the foil that will be the back of the head, make an indentation by pushing the back of the foil up with your thumbs to form the base of the head.

4. Make four ovals of clay about two inches long. Place them on all sides of the foil ball.

5. Smooth clay over foil to form the head. Leave the indentation at the back of the head because it will be used to form the jaw line.

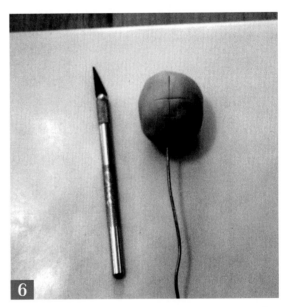

Sculpting the Face

6. Using an X-acto® knife, divide the face in half by drawing a light vertical line down the center. About halfway down the face, draw a horizontal line for the eyes. Divide that distance with the bottom of the face (chin) and draw a horizontal line for the nose. Divide the nose line and the chin by another horizontal line which will eventually form the mouth.

7. Using your thumbs, depress the clay along the horizontal eye line for the eye sockets. Leave a space for the nosebone in between. Place two small oval pads of clay in each eye socket for upper and lower lids.

8. Blend clay around the eye by first using the blunt edged tool. Next, use your thumbs to smooth the clay. Try to concentrate on the small area in the socket in order to retain the eyebrow bone.

9. With an X-acto® knife, draw horizontal slits through the smoothed ovals of clay. Add a small, thin strip of clay for the nosebone.

10. Elaborate on the eye line using the X-acto® knife. Add a whimsical look by dipping down at the inner edge of eyelids and curving up at the outer edge. Draw a large half circle for the mouth opening.

11. With the flat side of the X-acto® knife, push the upper lip of the mouth up and press the bottom lip down by putting pressure on the flat side of the knife. Insert into the mouth a very thin strip of clay for the upper teeth. Blend it in with blunt tool.

12. Start fleshing out the face. Add thin circles of clay to the cheeks and the area between the nose and mouth. Add a thin strip of clay for the lower half of the face and then a small circle for the chin.

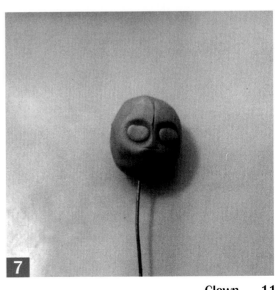

13. Blend the circles on face together by using the blunt tool and then smoothing with your fingers. Open the mouth a little more with the X-acto® knife and add a small oval of clay to the lower mouth for the tongue. With the blunt tool, make a small indentation vertically down the center of the tongue. Add a strip of clay for the neck and blend. Hold the neck as you continue to work.

14. Exaggerate the cheeks more by adding another two ovals of clay to the center of the existing cheeks. Blend with a blunt tool and then fingers, if necessary.

Teeth

15. Using an X-acto® knife, place a strip of clay in the upper part of the mouth. Mark the center of the strip with a light vertical line. Make another line on each side of the center line for the center of the front teeth. Keep in mind that the size and place ment of the teeth should be determined by the size of the mouth. Too many or not enough teeth will cause it to look dis-orted. Look in the mirror and notice the placement of your teeth. With the blunt tool, gently go around the perimeter of each tooth and round it out. Note that the two eye teeth on each side of the center front teeth are slightly pointed. When rounding out the other teeth, use the blunt tool to push one or two back to create realism. Shorten the teeth in the back by pushing the clay up with the blunt tool or the flat edge of the X-acto® knife. This creates a fading effect in the back of the mouth.

Nose

16. Decide how big you would like the nose. Shape a small ball of clay. Put it up to the face and see if it looks like a fit. When you are satisfied with the size you have chosen, attach the nose by blending the edges of the clay ball with the blunt tool.

13

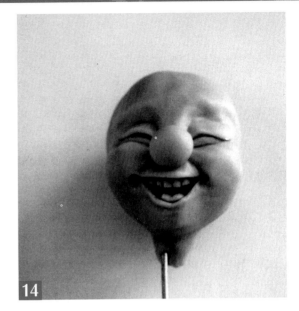

14

Finishing the Face

17. Add a dimple to each corner of the mouth with the round end of the blunt tool. With a finer, pointed tool, define the cheek and upper mouth area by drawing a light line from nose to mouth. Do the same for the area under the eye that is just above cheek. Using the blunt tool, add pressure to the lines as you are blending to define the areas you want to bring out.

Ears and Neck

18. The ear is aligned between the eyebrow and the end of the nose. Using the X-acto® knife, draw a light vertical line between these two points. Make two small ovals of clay the length of the lines. Put the ovals up to the line and turn the head from side to side to make sure of the placement. If the ears are down too far or up too high, the head will look distorted.

19. Take a good look at someone's ear. When you're sculpting, have a mirror ready to glance at your own ear as you go along. Attach the ear to the doll head. Secure and smooth the ear with the blunt tool.

20. With the same tool, make a very small hole that resembles a half moon in the center of the ear. Between the earhole and outer edge of ear line, make another half moon indentation with blunt tool. Make the rim around the outer edge of the ear. Add a tiny round piece of clay to form the protective lobe in the front of the center hole. Make a small oval pad for ear lobe and attach with blunt tool.

21. Finish the ear by turning the head to the side. Add a very thin vertical clay strip to the back between the head and ear and blend.

22. Start building up the neck by adding a strip of clay to the already existing strip. Blend it up into the back of the head and jaw line with the blunt tool. Add strips of clay and keep blending until you create a neck that suits the head; too thin or

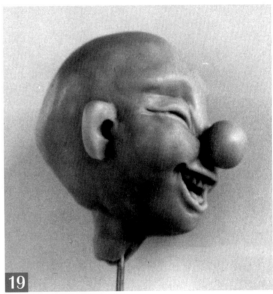

19

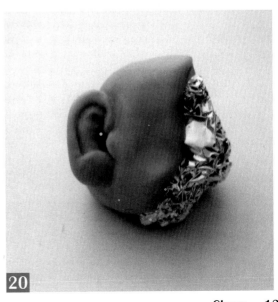

20

Clown

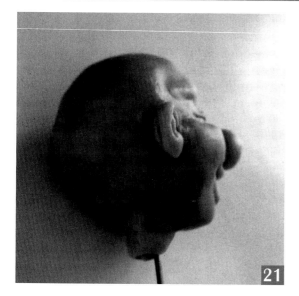

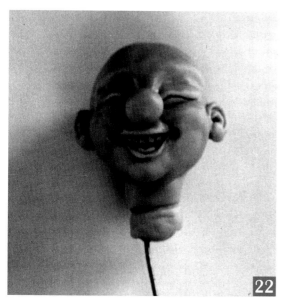

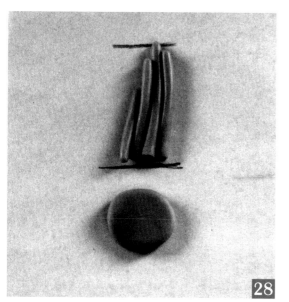

too fat will distort the doll. After you are satisfied with the neck, make a ring around the base with the blunt tool. This will form the ridge that will hold the glue used to adhere the muslin body pattern to the neck.

Finishing

23. Slightly bring out the chin a bit more by adding a small clay ball and blending well. With the blunt tool, make an indentation under the chin to define the chin line more clearly.
24. Move the head back and forth and make sure you are happy with the head from all angles. Smooth over any rough spots with your fingers or the blunt tool. You may want to dampen a Q-tip with water and go over the face in order to ensure extra smoothness.

Curing

25. Cover a small broiler pan with foil and place the head on it. Preheat the oven to 275 degrees. Place the head in the oven and time it for 15 minutes. Check the piece every 10 minutes thereafter until it is done. Always ventilate when curing clay!
26. When the head is cured, remove it from the oven and place it on a cooling rack until it has completely cooled.

Hands

27. To measure for the size of the hands, put the head on a piece of paper. Draw two horizontal lines on the paper, one next to the middle of the forehead and another next to the chin. Remove the head from the paper.
28. Starting with the middle finger, roll out a thin piece of clay and place it on the diagram between the two lines. Roll three other pieces of clay of similar size. Look at your own fingers and determine the different lengths. With the X-acto® knife, cut down fingers according to the appropriate size. Leave the middle finger where it is on the diagram. Take a tiny bit of clay off the index finger because that is the next longest. The ring finger is shorter than the middle finger and the index finger. The pinkie finger is between the center and the top of the ring finger.
29. Make a small circle of clay for the back of the hand. Put the small circle of clay over one-quarter of the bottom of the shaped fingers to create the outer part of the hand.
30. Take a 10 inch strand of wire and cover one-quarter of the wire with a small cylinder of clay to form the forearm. Make a paddle on the end of the wire for the palm of the hand.
31. Put the palm and back of hand (step 29) together. Blend with blunt tool and use your fingers to smooth.
32. Flesh out fingers by placing thin strips of clay over fingers. Blend with blunt tool until they look like real fingers. Turn the hand frequently, working to flesh out the palm side as well.
33. Roll a very small cylinder of clay for the thumb. Look at your

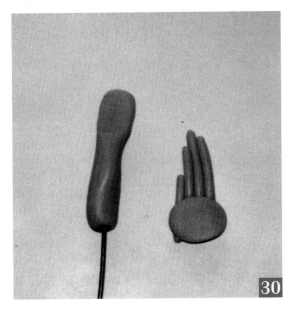

30

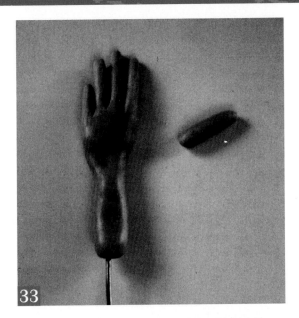

33

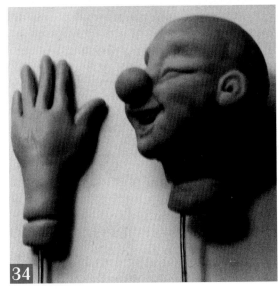

34

own thumb for placement. Attach the thumb to the index finger side of hand. It should be placed lower down on the hand and not too near the index finger. Blend with your blunt tool to secure it.

34. Shape the thumb to look real by bending it out from the hand slightly. Add a ridge at the bottom of the forearm for when you will attach the muslin body. Put the hand next to the head again to make sure it is the correct proportion.

35. Make the other hand the same way, except reverse the fingers. When you are rolling out the fingers and placing them, have the already sculpted hand near you to be sure you are making the opposite hand and it is the same size.

36. When you have finished the other hand, make sure they are a matching pair in size and shape. You may want to pose them or leave them straight. The type of doll you are making will determine the pose. For instance, if you have already decided that you would like the doll to hold a bouquet of flowers, pose the fingers in a grip position. I left the clown hands out stretched for a welcoming effect.

37. Sign the doll. With the sharp tool, carve your initials in the palm, an abbreviated date and a small copyright symbol ©.

38. Bake the hands in the oven on a foil covered pan at 275 degrees. Watch the hands every 10 minutes because they are thin and may cook quickly. When the hands are cured, remove them from the oven and cool them on a cooling rack.

Legs and Shoes

39. The measurements for the shoes of this clown will be exaggerated. Place a piece of cardboard under the head to get an idea of what would be a normal shoe measurement. Using the head as a guide, measure from the top of the forehead to the chin. Since we are making larger shoes, outline with a pen or pencil from the top of the head to the end of the neck or even a little longer.

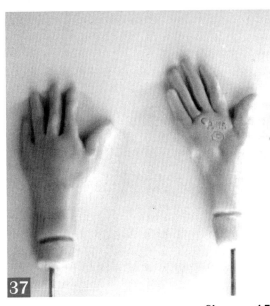

37

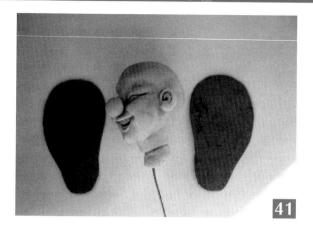

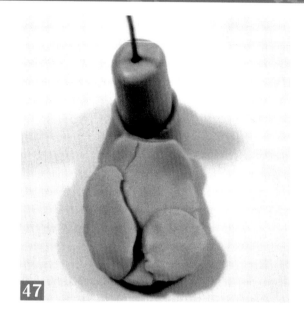

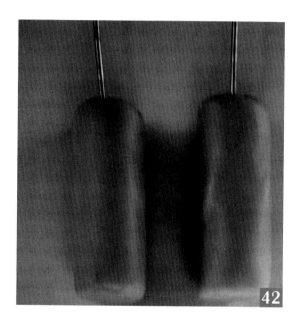

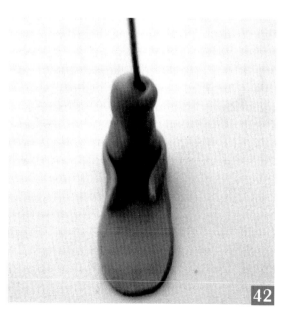

40. Using the drawing as a guide, shape the shoe, giving it a straight inside edge, a round outer edge and a narrow heel. Mark the inside so you will know the left from the right. Cut out the shoe pattern and place it face down on the cardboard. Trace, draw, and cut out the other shoe. Mark "inside" on the opposite shoe.

41. Put the shoe pattern next to the head to be sure it is not too large. Check to make sure you have a left and right shoe pattern.

42. Roll out two cylinders of clay for the lower half of the leg. Make the stumps thick enough to provide stability. They will be helping to hold the weight of the entire doll so they can not be too thin. Use two, 10 inch strands of wire and put them through the middle of the cylinder. Do not go all the way through to the bottom or it will continue to protrude through the shoe.

43. Use a rolling pin to roll out a flat piece of clay about 1/4 inch thick. Put the cardboard shoe patterns on the flat piece of clay and trace it lightly with the sharp tool. Take the pattern off the clay and use the X-acto® knife to cut them out. These will be the soles of the shoes.

44. Bake these clay soles in the oven on a foil covered baking pan at 275 degrees. Since the soles are thin, watch the clay every 10 minutes. When soles are cured, put them on a cooling rack and let them cool.

45. Using the cardboard sole of the shoe pattern, follow the directions in step #43 and cut out two more clay soles. Do not bake these, they will be the upper part of the shoe.

46. Take the wired clay cylinder of the lower leg and put it on the heel part of the shoe. Mold a thin strip of clay for the back of the shoe. Attach it to the cylinder and the flat sole of clay. This should help hold the lower leg in place while you shape the shoe.

47. Start shaping the body of the shoe with pieces of clay. You

may want to put the cardboard soles under the upper part of the shoe for support while you work. Think of the big toe, the small toes, and the tongue of shoe when shaping the pieces of clay. Do the same for the other shoe but reverse the details. Blend all pieces together with blunt tool and then smooth them with your fingers. If you have used the cardboard soles, remove them and replace with the baked clay soles. Blend the upper body of the shoe with the soles. With the sharp edged tool, draw a line around the shoe to separate the sole from the upper shoe.

48. Make ridges at the top of the lower legs to attach armature.

49. To decorate the shoes, make flaps of clay for each side of the shoe and attach them to the body. Blend them together. Outline the tongue with the sharp tool and then round the tops. Use the blunt tool to make holes for laces on the flaps of the shoe. Make the holes deep enough to create a well to hold glue and shoelaces.

50. Bake in oven on a foil covered baking pan at 275 degrees. Check after 15 minutes and then every 10 minutes after that. When cured, let cool on cooling rack.

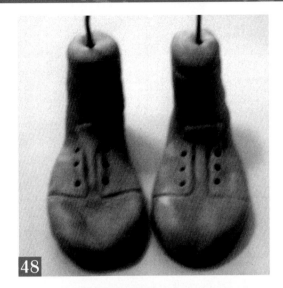

Armature

Refer to the Scale section and the Adult Figure Sketch. This is the guide you will be working from for measuring the armature.

51. Take two, 12 inch wire strands and twist them together for the torso. Leave the top and bottom of the wire untwisted so that you can bend the wire to form the arms and legs.

52. Attach the head to the torso by twisting the head wire to the torso armature and securing with pliers.

53. To determine the height of the doll, take the head measurement from the chin to the forehead and multiply by 8. We are using the numeral 8 because proportionally, an average adult doll will stand 7 1/2 to 8 heads high. For example, my doll's head measures 2 inches. Multiplying that by 8 yields 16. So, 16 inches will be the height of the doll.

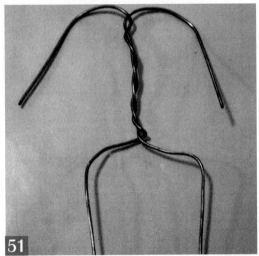

Arm and Leg Pattern

All of the pattern pieces are marked and ready for use. Before using these pattern pieces, always check them against your own doll. Since you are making an original doll, your measurements may not be the same as mine so you may have to alter these patterns.

54. Cut out four 8x5 inch pieces of muslin for the arms and legs. The width and length of the muslin are only an approximation at this point. Place the forearm part of the armature on the edge of the muslin. Place the lower leg armature close to the muslin edge. Do this for all four pieces of armature.

55. Fold the muslin over the armature.

56. Go back to the sketch and measure the arm on the figure from the top of the shoulder to the hand. It should measure about 6

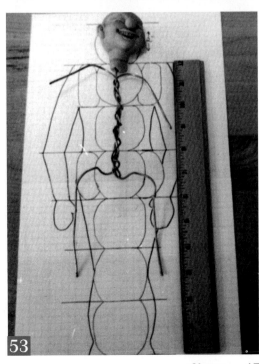

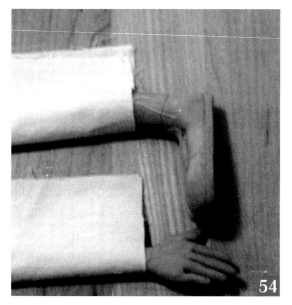

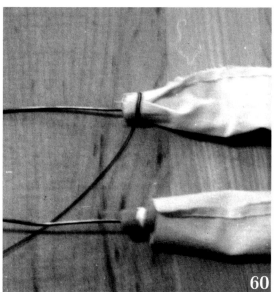

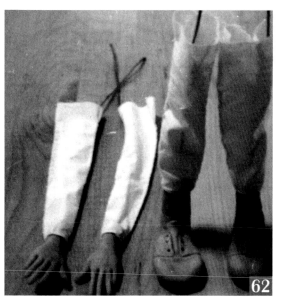

inches. You will need extra length for sewing and attaching the armature to the torso. A measurement of about 7-1/4 inches will give you enough length to work with. It is better to have to shorten the pattern than to have to start over. This measurement will be fine for the legs as well. Measure the width of the muslin and leave about 1/2 inch extra muslin for sewing the seams on the pattern.

57. Put the ruler on the wrist about 1/4 inch away from clay and mark it with a dot. Draw a diagonal line from that point to the top edge of the muslin. This will create a thinner section for the forearm and wider section as you go up the arm. The leg pattern pieces can be straighter and wider because the upper leg is heavier and the added weight will help the finished doll stand alone.

58. Cut the muslin arm pattern to size. Before sewing these pieces, put the muslin arm and leg pieces on a piece of card board and trace it (*see Clown Arm and Leg Pattern*). Mark it and cut it out for future use. With a sewing machine, stitch all four pieces leaving 1/4 inch seam allowance.

Attaching Muslin to Arm and Leg Armature

59. Attach the muslin to the sculpted arms and legs by pulling the muslin over each of the arms and legs so that the wrong side of the muslin is facing out. Pull the muslin down just below the ridges. Make sure the seams of the muslin are in the back of the legs and the palm side of the hands.

60. Fill the ridges of the armature with glue. Pull the muslin up over the glued ridges. The muslin will not fit tightly over the wrist ridges. Overlap excess material on each side of the seam in the back. This will create a dart. Make sure the excess material is facing the center of seam. Secure the muslin to the armature with a small piece of thin wire (floral wire works well).

61. Let the pieces dry.

62. When glue has dried, pull the muslin up, so it is right side out, to form the cloth part of the arms and legs.

63. Pin along the lines of those limbs that had excess material folded toward the center seam and sew. This method will allow you to "sculpt" the material and thin out whatever you feel is too thick.

Assembling the Armature

64. Using the *Adult Figure Sketch* as a guide, match the leg armature to the drawing. Let the shoes fall below the last line. Twist the leg wires around the torso wire armature and secure the wire with pliers.

65. Once the legs are in place, put the piece back on the *Adult Figure Sketch* and place the arms where they should fall using the sketch as a guide. Twist the arm wires around the top of the torso wire armature and secure it with pliers.

66. Wrap the wire with masking tape. This will soften and help pad the armature for stuffing.

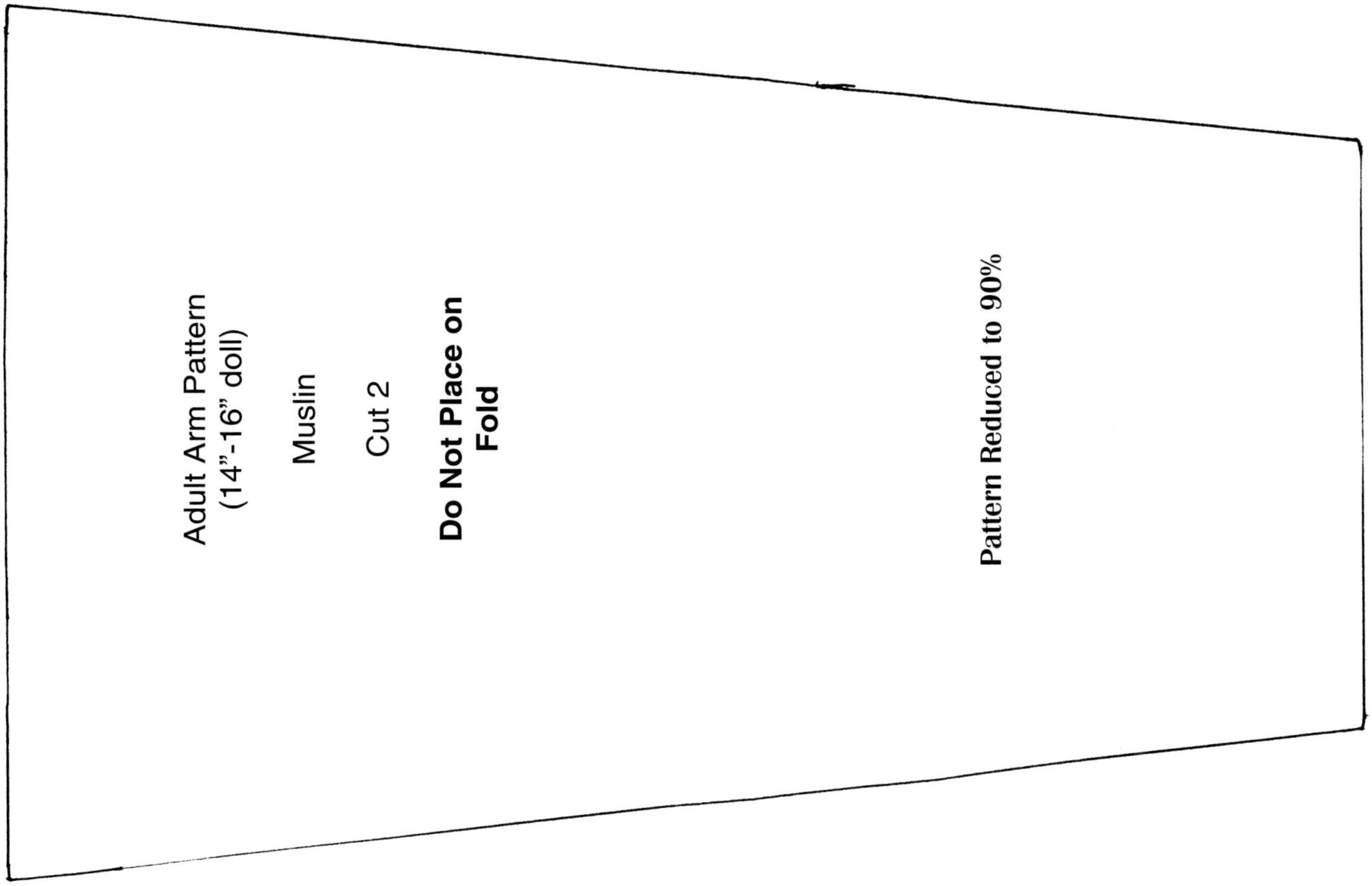

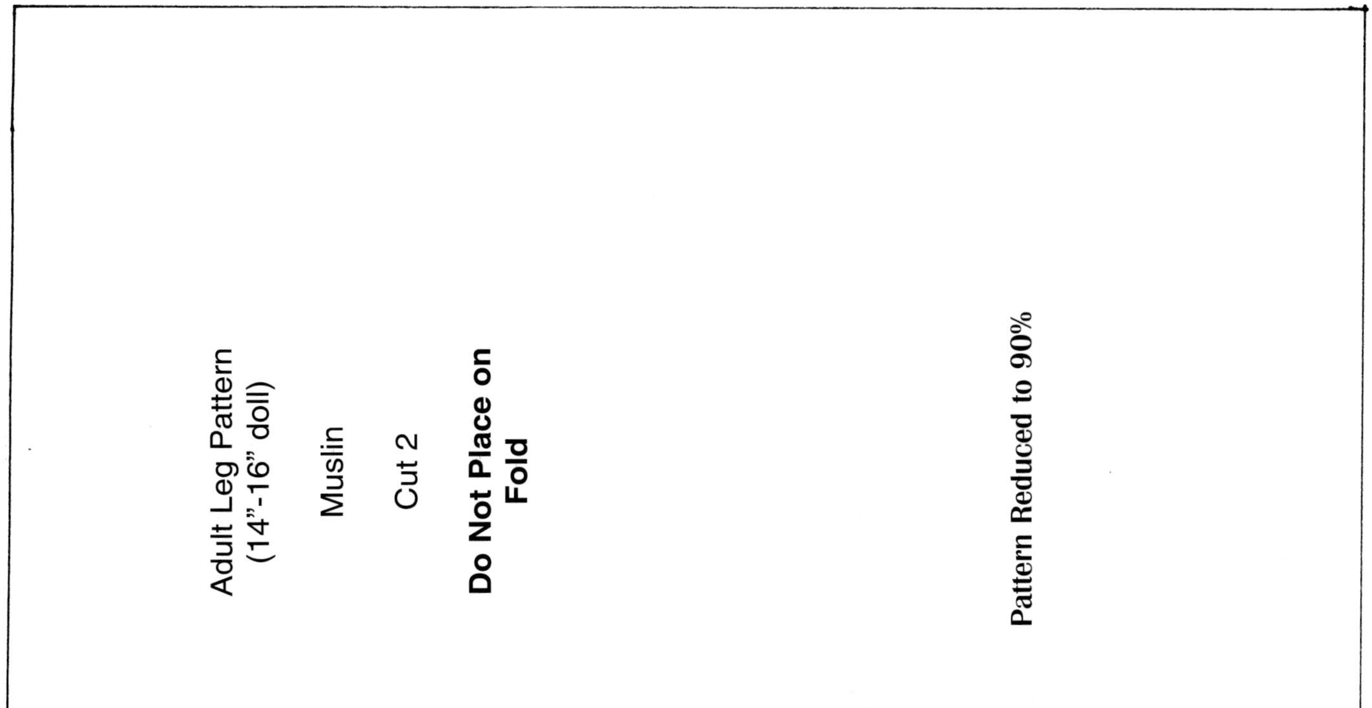

Adult Arm Pattern
(14"-16" doll)

Muslin

Cut 2

**Do Not Place on
Fold**

Pattern Reduced to 90%

Adult Leg Pattern
(14"-16" doll)

Muslin

Cut 2

**Do Not Place on
Fold**

Pattern Reduced to 90%

Pattern Reduced to 90%

Clown

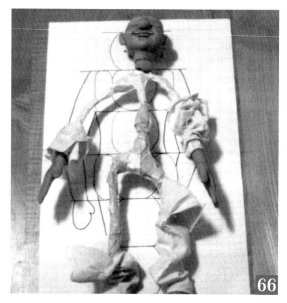

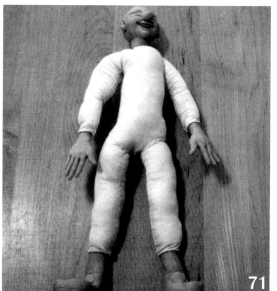

Stuffing the Body

67. Stuff the arms and legs with polyester batting. Use a thin dowel stick or a pencil to firmly and evenly stuff all the limbs. Wrap a strip of quilt batting around the torso armature to flesh it out a little. This will aid in Making the body pattern.

Torso Pattern

68. Place wax paper or tracing paper over the *Adult Figure Sketch* and draw the body from the top of the shoulders to just below the hips. Remove the paper from the sketch and cut it out.

69. Transfer this pattern to graph paper and add 1/4 inch on all sides for seam allowances. Cut out the pattern and mark it (see *Clown Body Pattern*). Transfer the pattern to muslin and cut two out, for the front and the back.

70. Sew the shoulder and side seams leaving 1/4 inch seam allowances. Turn the pattern to the right side and at the center of the neck edge on one pattern piece only cut a line about 1-1/2 inches down. This will be the back of the pattern and the opening will allow you to get the pattern over the doll.

71. Pull the muslin pattern over the doll and use the leg, arm, and neck openings to stuff the torso part of the doll. Hand sew around the leg and arm openings. Around the ridge, sew the neck and back opening closed .

Painting

72. Using acrylic paint, paint a white mask on the clown's face from the forehead to the chin (do not include ears). Paint all of the hands white. I have chosen black for the eyebrows and red for the nose and mouth. The teeth are a mixture of white and yellow. Let the paint dry. Apply a matte finish to the face to seal the paint.

73. Using acrylic paint, paint the side flaps and soles of the shoes black. The upper body of the shoe is painted a putty color to match the costume. Mix brown and black paint to smudge parts of the shoe on top and around the sides. Let the paint dry. Apply a matte finish to the tops and bottoms of the shoes to protect them from chipping.

74. The laces of the shoes are made from the fringe of trim. Cut individual strands of fringe. With a toothpick, dab lace holes with glue and put one strand of fringe in each hole and lace diagonally up the shoe. Leave the top strands of fringe free for tying. Let them dry and then tie the laces.

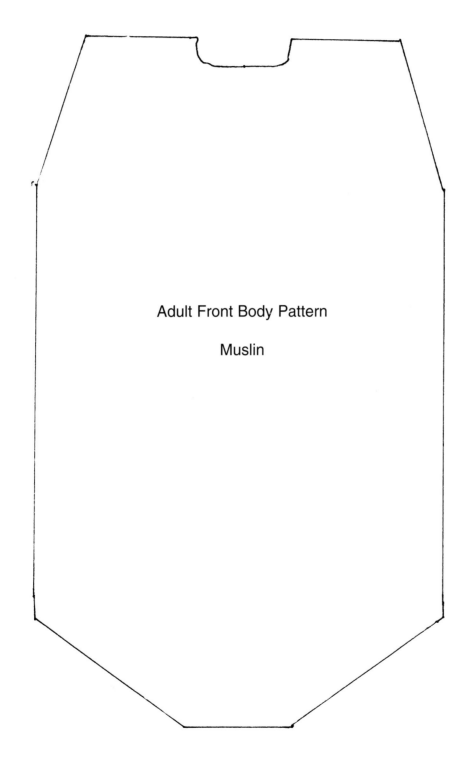

Adult Front Body Pattern

Muslin

Clown

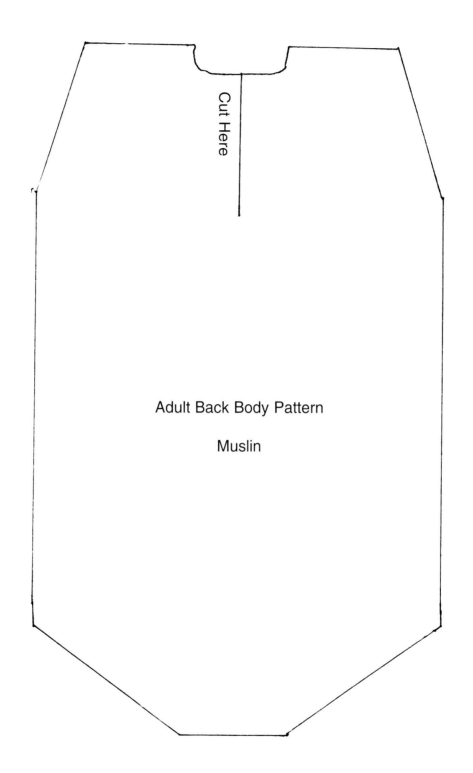

Cut Here

Adult Back Body Pattern

Muslin

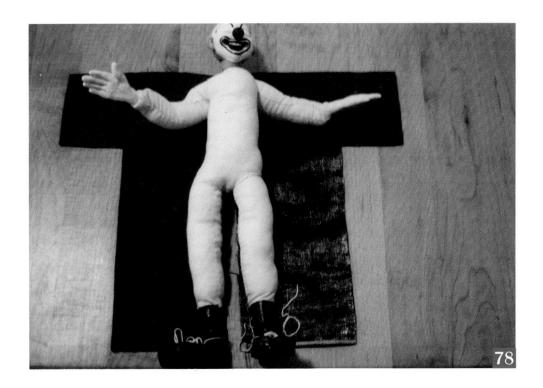

78

Costume

75. Place the whole body of the clown on graph paper. Extend an arm out. Leave extra space on each side of the body for the balloon effect and extra length at wrists and ankles for hemming (see *Clown Costume Pattern—page 31*). Sketch this on graph paper.
76. Cut out the pattern and mark it.
77. Choose two different colored pieces of material that complement each other. The material should not be too stiff since it needs to fall and look blousey. Knits and shiny materials work fine. If the material has a pattern, make sure it is not too big for the scale of the doll. Use the graph paper pattern to cut the costume out. Cut four pieces—two of each color.
78. Place the doll between both sides of the material. Mark the material with a pin about 2 inches down from the crotch. This is where you will join the material to leave enough room for sitting and positioning of doll.
79. Leaving a 1/4 inch seam allowance, sew the outer "L" shape of the costume from the ankle to the wrist on each side. Sew from the wrist to the shoulder seams, leaving a loose neck edge. Sew the individual leg openings, on both sides, up to the pin mark which is below the crotch. Sew the front and back together.
    Start at the front neck edge, continue down around the crotch, and up the back to within about 2 inches of the top back of neck. That opening will enable you to get the costume on the clown.
80. Put the costume on the doll. Turn under the raw edges at the neck, wrist, and ankle openings. Use a running stitch, gathered tightly, to sew these openings closed. Use a decorative matching trim to sew around the neck and the wrists.

Hat

81. Cut an oval cardboard for the brim of the clown hat about the size of the clown's head (see *Clown Brim Hat Pattern—#81*). To measure for the size, start with a small hole in the center of the oval and keep placing it on top of the clown's head until it is large enough to cover part of the head.
82. Roll out a flat piece of clay and trace the cardboard pattern on the clay. Cut out the pattern with the X-acto® knife. Roll out another flat piece of clay; a little larger than the clay oval in the center of the hat brim. Find the center of this piece and fold each side of the clay into the center to form an indentation for the top of the hat.

Clown

Neck—do not sew

Cut on line
for back
piece only

Clown Front & Back Costume

Cut 4

(2 of each color if different)

Pattern Reduced to 50%

Crotch

Inner Leg Seams

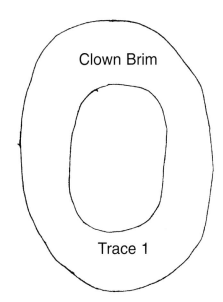

Clown Brim

Trace 1

Pattern Reduced to 50%

82

87

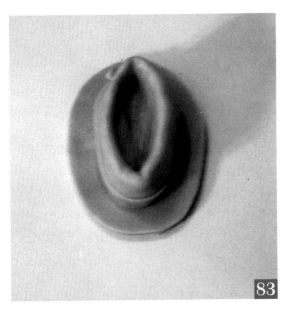

83

Roll out a flat strip of clay for the band around the side of the hat. Measure it against the center oval to determine the length and join them together. Roll out another thin strip of clay for the decorative band around the hat.

83. Place the side band on top of the clay oval brim of the hat and blend those two pieces together with the blunt tool. Place the indented clay oval (which is the top of the hat) on top of the brim and blend those two pieces together. Smooth the hat with your fingers. Place the decorative band around the side of the hat and blend.

84. Bake hat in oven on a foil covered baking pan for 275 degrees. Check clay every 10 minutes. Let it cool on a cooling rack.

85. Paint the hat with a metallic finish and sprinkle sparkle on the wet paint. Use a complementary color for the brim. Let it dry. Use a matte finish on the hat to prevent it from chipping. Decorate the side of the hat by gluing on tiny silk flowers and a feather.

Hair

86. Use a hot glue gun to apply hair to the head. I chose red mohair. Cut a section of hair about 4 inches long. Place the doll face down to apply the hair.

87. Make a ring with the hot glue gun around the head which is below the white mask line and a little above the ear. Work quickly because the hot glue dries very quickly. Place the edge of the mohair all around the ring. Bend the hair down so it curves over the glue ring. Let it dry.

Finishing

88. Place the hat on top of the head at an angle. Remove it and turn it over. Use a hot glue gun around the inside rim of the hat where it will sit on the head. Place the hat back on the head. ■

85

This project will refine some of the features you learned in the Clown project. You will detail more of the face by inserting glass eyes, defining the nose and adding wrinkles and crevices to the face and hands. You'll learn to make eyeglasses and fingernails, as well as jewelry, stockings and other accessories.

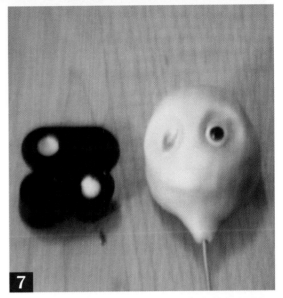

Beginning the Body
1. Cut six strands of wire about 10 inches long for the legs, arms, head and torso. Cut two strands of wire about 12 inches long for the torso armature.

Beginning the Head
2. Make a small ball out of foil and run a 10 inch strand of wire through it. Extend a little of the wire over the top of the foil. With pliers, bend the top of the wire to make a hook and push it back down into the foil to bury and secure it. (See *Clown—Beginning the Head #2*).
3. On the side of the foil that will be the back of the head, make an indentation by pushing the back of the foil up with your thumbs to form the base of the head.
4. Make four ovals of clay about 2 inches long. Place them on all sides of the foil ball. Smooth clay over the foil to form the head. Leave the indentation at the back of the head which forms the jaw line.

Sculpting the Face
5. Using an X-acto® knife, divide the face in half by drawing a light vertical line down the center (see *Clown—Sculpting the Face #6*). About halfway down the face, draw a horizontal line for the eyes. Divide that distance with the bottom of the face (chin) and draw a horizontal line for the nose. Divide the nose line and the chin by another horizontal line which will eventually form the mouth.
6. Using your thumbs, depress the clay along the horizontal eye line for the eye sockets. Leave space for nose bone in between.
7. Using the blunt tool, make a deep puncture in each eye socket for the eyes. I used 8mm glass brown eyes. Insert the eyes in the holes. Have the eyes facing in a downward position. Make sure they are both focused in the same direction.
8. Roll out four small pieces of clay for the upper and lower lids. Since this doll will be looking down, make the upper lids a little wider than the lower to show more of the top eyelid. Using a blunt tool, blend the upper lids into eye sockets being careful not to touch the brow bone. Place the lower lids on the eyes and blend them into the face.
9. Start building the forehead by placing a thin strip of clay horizontally above the eyebrows. Round out the area around the temples with your fingers. Place a thin strip of clay vertically

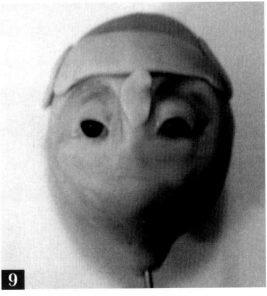

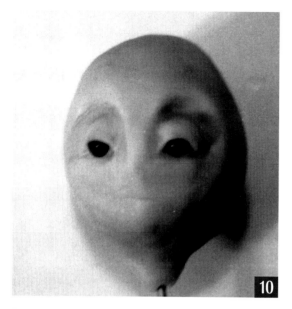

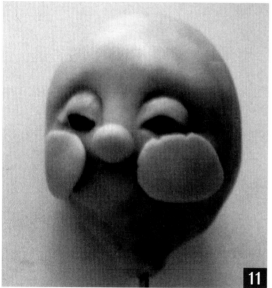

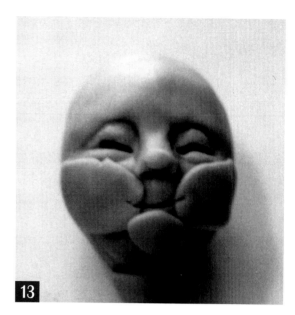

down from the forehead for the bridge of the nose.

10. Use a blunt tool to blend these pieces together. Keep the emphasis on the eyebrow bone as you work to define that portion of the face.

11. Make a small ball of clay for the nose and two small circles for the cheeks. With the blunt tool, blend the ball of the nose up into the bridge. Blend the cheeks into the face.

12. Add small pieces of clay under the eyes. Blend these pieces so they cover quite a bit of the lower half of the eye. Fill in the area between the nose and the upper mouth with a small piece of clay to round out the upper lip area. Start shaping the chin by rolling out a longer piece of clay to fit across the bottom half of the face and then a smaller piece of clay for the chin accent. Blend everything together with the blunt tool and then smooth it with your fingers.

13. With the sharper pointed tool, make holes for nostrils. Add more rounded circles of clay for the cheeks and chin. Use the X-acto® knife to make a smile line for the mouth. Add a tiny circle of clay at the tip of the nose for a better shape. Do not sculpt and smooth the features yet.

14. Roll out a strip of clay for the neck and place it under the chin Hold the neck while sculpting and smoothing the lower half of the face to avoid disturbing the facial features already in place.

15. Flair out the nostrils in the nose by placing the blunt tool inside the nostril and moving it in a circular motion.

16. Start drawing the lines in the face with the sharp pointed tool. Draw horizontal lines across the forehead, at the corners of the eyes, and around the cheek area from the nose to the mouth.

17. Add a tiny strip of clay for the lower lip and a small round circle of clay for the chin. Blend it with a blunt tool and smooth with your fingers.

18. With the side of the blunt tool, define the upper lips by empha-sizing upper points on the center of the lips. Add a tiny piece

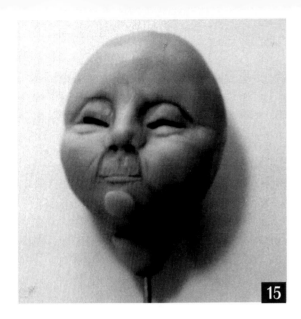

15

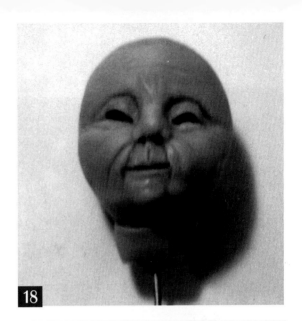

18

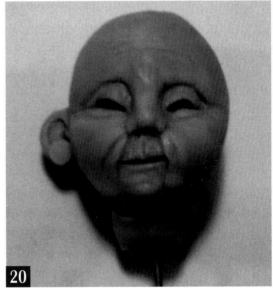

20

of clay between the nostrils for the septum. Draw a pronounced line down from the nose to the mouth. Make jowls on each side of the chin by adding tiny pieces of clay to each side of the chin and blending them with your fingers. Add more crevices in the cheeks and fine lines all over the face. Add another strip of clay to the neck.

Ears and Neck

19. The ear is placed between the eyebrow and the end of the nose at the side of the head (see *Clown—Placement of Ear #18*). Using the X-acto® knife, draw a light vertical line between these two points. Make two small ovals of clay the length of the lines. Put the ovals up to the line and turn the head from side to side to make sure of the placement. If the ears are down too far or up too high, they will draw unwanted attention to that area of the head.

20. Take a good look at someone's ear. When you are sculpting, have a mirror ready to glance at your own ear as you go along. Attach the ear to the head (see *Clown—Placement of Ear #19*). Secure and smooth the ear with the blunt tool.

21. With the same tool, in the center of the ear make a very small hole that resembles a half moon. Add a tiny round piece of clay to form the protective lobe in the front of the center hole. Use the blunt tool to make the rim around the outer edge of the ear. Draw a half moon from the upper earhole to the bottom where the lobe will be placed. Between the earhole and the outer edge of ear line, make another half moon indentation with the blunt tool. Make a small oval pad for each ear lobe and attach it with the blunt tool.

22. Elongate the ear lobe by adding more clay to the bottom of lobe.

23. Turn the head to the side to finish the ear. Add a very thin vertical clay strip to the back between the head and the ear. Then blend them together.

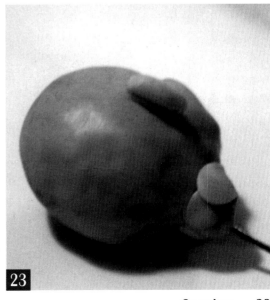

23

25

24. Make a hole for the earrings by driving a thin piece of floral wire through the lobe.
25. Blend the strips of clay around the neck into the back of the head, jaw and chin line with the blunt tool. A neck that is too thin or too fat will distort the doll. Make wrinkles in the neck by adding tiny bits of clay to the neck and blending them with the blunt tool.
26. After you are satisfied with the neck, make a ring around the base of it with the blunt tool. This will form the ridge to hold the glue which will adhere the muslin body pattern to the neck.

Curing
27. Cover a small broiler pan with foil and place the head on it. Preheat the oven to 275 degrees. Set timer for 15 minutes. Check oven at 10 minute intervals until piece is baked.
28. When the head is cured, remove it from the oven and let it stand on a cooling rack until it is completely cooled.

Hands
29. To measure for the size of the hands, put the head on a piece of paper. Draw two horizontal lines on the paper, one next to the middle of the forehead and another next to the chin. Remove the head from the paper.
30. Starting with the middle finger, roll out a thin piece of clay and place it on the diagram between the lines (see *Clown—Hands* #28). Roll three other pieces of clay of similar size. Look at your own fingers and determine the different lengths. With an X-acto® knife, cut down fingers according to size. Leave the middle finger where it is on the diagram. Take a tiny bit of clay off the index finger since that is the next longest. The ring finger is shorter than the middle and index finger. The pinkie finger is between the center and top of the ring finger. Make a small circle of clay for the back of the hand.

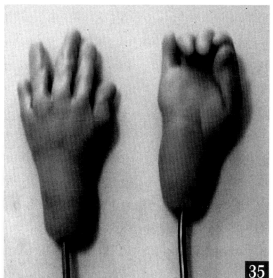

35

31. Take a 10 inch strand of wire and cover 1/4 of the wire with a small cylinder of clay to form the forearm (see *Clown—Hands* #30). Make a paddle on the end of the wire for the palm of the hand. Put a small circle of clay over 1/4 of the bottom of the shaped fingers to create the outer part of the hand.
32. Put the palm and the back of hand together. Blend them together with the blunt tool and use your fingers to smooth.
33. Flesh out the fingers by placing thin strips of clay over them. Blend with the blunt tool until they look like real fingers. Turn the hand frequently, working to flesh out the palm side as well.
34. Roll a very small cylinder of clay for the thumb (see *Clown—Hands* #33). Look at your own thumb for placement. Attach the thumb on the index finger side of the hand. It should be placed lower down the hand and not too near the index finger. Blend with the blunt tool and shape to make it look real.
35. Make the other hand the same way, except reverse the fingers.

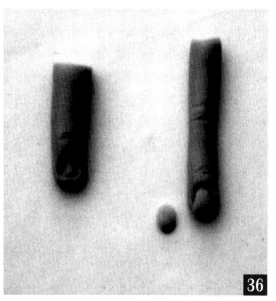

36

When you are rolling out the fingers and placing them, have the already sculpted hand near you so you can be sure you are making the opposite hand. Put the hand next to the head again to make sure of correct measurement. You may want to pose the hands. I have spaced out the fingers on one hand and bent the fingers on the other.

36. Use your own hands as a guide in determining the placement of nails, knuckles and wrinkles. Use the sharp pointed tool for the nails. For example, starting at the tip of the finger, draw a nail. Go back around the sides and indent the nail so it stands out in clay. Lift the tip of the nail a bit for a more rounded effect.

37. Use the X-acto® knife to carve the lines for the knuckles. Start in the middle of the finger and draw a short line. Keep adding lines around the center of the finger until you have created a real looking knuckle. Look at the lines and creases on your hands and recreate them for the doll's hand. With the blunt tool, draw lines for veins and wrinkles from the wrist to the fingers. This will emphasize the age of the doll.

38. Sign the palm of the doll's hand or you may wish to wait and sign the bottom of the shoe. With the sharp tool, carve your initials, an abbreviated date, and a copyright symbol ©.

39. Add a ridge at the bottom of the forearm for attaching the muslin body.

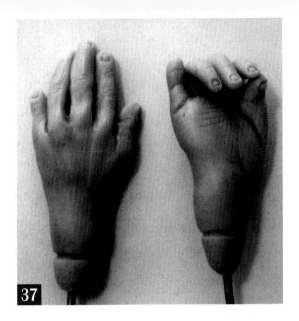

Ring

40. Pry the pinkie and the middle finger of the left hand a little away from the ring finger. Use a small piece of thin gold trim or wire and wrap it around the ring finger. Twist the wire on the inside of the doll's finger to secure it. Clip the excess with wire cutters or scissors. With the blunt tool, tuck the wire into the clay skin to cover it. Gently move fingers back into position.

41. Bake the hands in the oven on a foil covered pan at 275 degrees. Watch the hands every 10 minutes because they are thin and may cook quickly. When the hands are done, place them on a cooling rack.

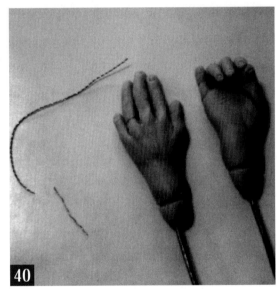

Legs and Slippers

42. Put the doll's head on a piece of paper and draw a horizontal line at the top of the forehead and at the chin. Remove the head from the paper.

43. Using these measurements as a guide for the shoes, draw a sketch of a shoe between these lines. Remember there is an inside and an outside edge and the heel is narrower. Mark the inside of the shoe so you will know the left from the right. Cut out this paper sole and trace it onto cardboard. Cut out the cardboard sole and place it face down on the cardboard again to create the other shoe. Trace, draw, and cut out the other shoe. Mark the "inside" on the opposite shoe (see *Grandma Shoe Pattern*).

Grandma Shoe Pattern

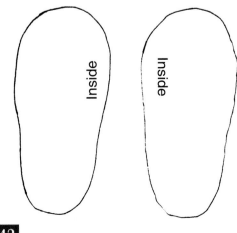

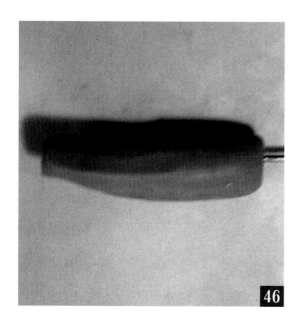 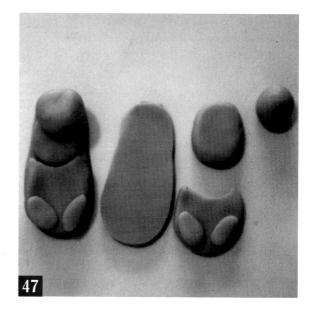

44. Use a rolling pin to roll out a flat piece of clay about 1/4 inch thick. Put the cardboard shoe pattern on the flat piece of clay and trace it lightly with the sharp tool. Take the pattern off the clay and use the X-acto® knife to cut them out. These will be the soles of the shoes.

45. Roll out two cylinders of clay for the lower half of the leg. Make stumps thick enough to provide stability for they will be helping to hold the weight of the entire doll. Use two, 10 inch strands of wire and put them through the middle of the cylinder. Do not go all the way to the bottom or it will protrude through the shoe.

46. Using your own lower leg as a guide, start carving the calf and ankle. Pare off excess clay with the X-acto® knife. Use your fingers as you go along to smooth the clay.

47. Start shaping the slipper. Roll out a flat piece of clay. Place the two cardboard sole shoe patterns on the clay. Trace the patterns with the sharp tool and cut them out with the X-acto® knife.

48. Roll out another piece of flat clay. Trace the two front portions of the soles of the slippers with the sharp pointed tool and cut them out with the X-acto® knife. Cut the inside edges into a half moon shape for the front portion of the slippers. Use four small ovals of clay for the big and small toes on each shoe. Position them on the tops of the half moons. These will be toe indentations in the shoes.

49. Roll out an oval of clay for the heel of the foot and a ball of clay for the ankle. Place the half moons of clay on the front part of the slippers. Fit the oval pieces of clay on top of the heel portions of the soles. Then, place the ankle balls on top of the oval.

50. Blend these pieces together with the blunt tool and then your fingers. Leave the oval defined all around the soles of slippers as it is the heel part of the foot. Leave a deep crevice where the ovals and half moons meet in the front of the slippers. This will be where the stockings are glued to the leg.

51. Blend the lower leg into the ankle. If necessary, add clay to the ankle to thicken and reinforce it. Make sure the slipper and the foot are clearly defined. Make a ridge at the top of the lower leg for attaching the muslin leg pat tern by taking the blunt tool and making a ring around the leg.

52. Bake the legs and shoes in the oven at 275 degrees on a foil covered broiler pan. Check the pieces after 15 minutes and every 10 minutes thereafter. When done, let cool on cooling rack.

Armature

Refer to Adult Figure Sketch. This is the guide you will be working from for measuring armature. Place the doll on the sketch to be sure your proportions match so far.

53. Take two 12 inch wire strands and twist them together for the torso (see *Clown—Armature* #51).

54. Attach the head to the torso by twisting the head wire to the torso armature. To determine the height of doll, take the head measurement from the chin to the forehead and multiply by 8. We are using the numeral 8 because proportionally, an average adult doll will stand 7 1/2 to 8 heads high. For example, my doll's head measure 2 inches. Multiplying that by 8 yields 16. So, 16 inches will be the height of my doll.

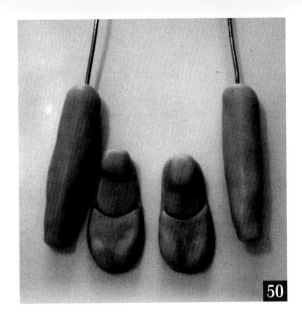

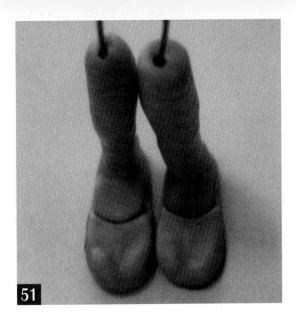

Arm and Leg Pattern

All of the pattern pieces are marked and ready for use. Before using these pattern pieces, always check them against your doll. Since you are making an original doll, your measurements may not be the same as mine; you may have to alter these patterns to fit your own creation.

55. Cut out four 8x5 inch pieces of muslin for the arms and legs. The width and length of the muslin are only an approximation at this point. Place the forearm part of the armature on the edge of the muslin. Place the lower leg armature close to the muslin edge. Do this for all four pieces of the armature.

56. Fold the muslin over the armature. The muslin should fall just below the knee.

57. Go back to the sketch and measure the arm on the figure from the top of the shoulder to the hand. It should measure about 6 inches. You will need extra length for sewing and attaching the armature to the torso. A measurement of about 7-1/4 inches will give you enough length to work with. It is better to shorten the pattern than have to start over. This measurement will be fine for the legs as well. Measure the width of the muslin and leave about 1/2 inch extra muslin for sewing the seams on the pattern.

58. Put the ruler on the wrist about 1/4 inch away from the clay and mark it with a dot. Draw a diagonal line from that point to the top edge of the muslin. This will create a thinner section for the forearm and a wider section as you go up the arm. The leg pattern pieces can be straighter and wider because the upper leg is heavier and the added weight will help the finished doll stand alone.

59. Cut the muslin arm pattern to size. Before sewing these pieces, put the arm and leg muslin on a piece of card board and trace it. Mark it and cut it out for future use (see *Grandma Arm and Leg Body Pattern-page 42*). With a sewing machine, stitch all four pieces leaving 1/4 inch seam allowance.

Attaching Muslin to Arm and Leg Armature

60. Attach the muslin pattern to the arm and leg armature by pulling the pieces over each of the arms and legs so that the wrong side of the muslin is facing out. Pull the material down just below the ridges. Make sure the seams of the muslin are in the back of the legs and the palm side of the hands.

61. Fill the ridges of the armature with glue (see *Clown—Attaching Muslin to Arm and Leg Armature* #60). Pull the muslin up over the glued ridges. The muslin will not fit tightly over the wrist ridges. Pull material on each side of the seam at the back and overlap like a dart. Make sure excess material is facing toward the center of the seam. Secure the muslin to the armature with a small piece of thin wire (floral wire works well).

62. Let the pieces dry.

63. When the glue has dried, pull the muslin up to form the cloth part of the arms and legs (see *Clown—Attaching Muslin to Arm and Leg Armature* #62).

64. Pin along the lines of those limbs that had excess material folded toward the center seam and sew. This method

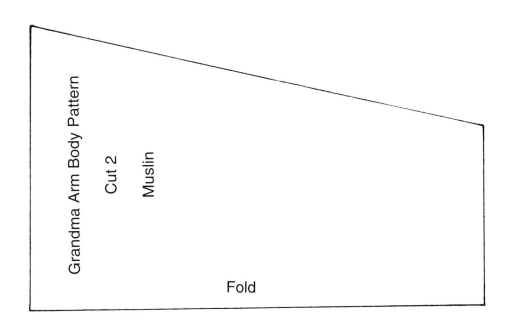

Grandma Arm Body Pattern

Cut 2

Muslin

Fold

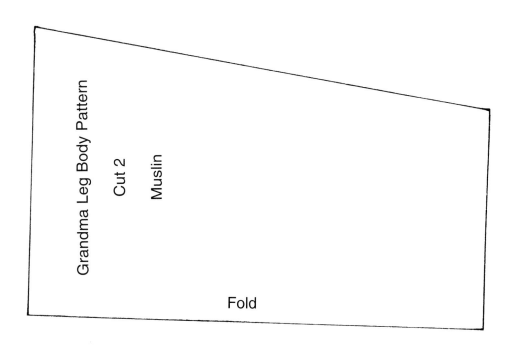

Grandma Leg Body Pattern

Cut 2

Muslin

Fold

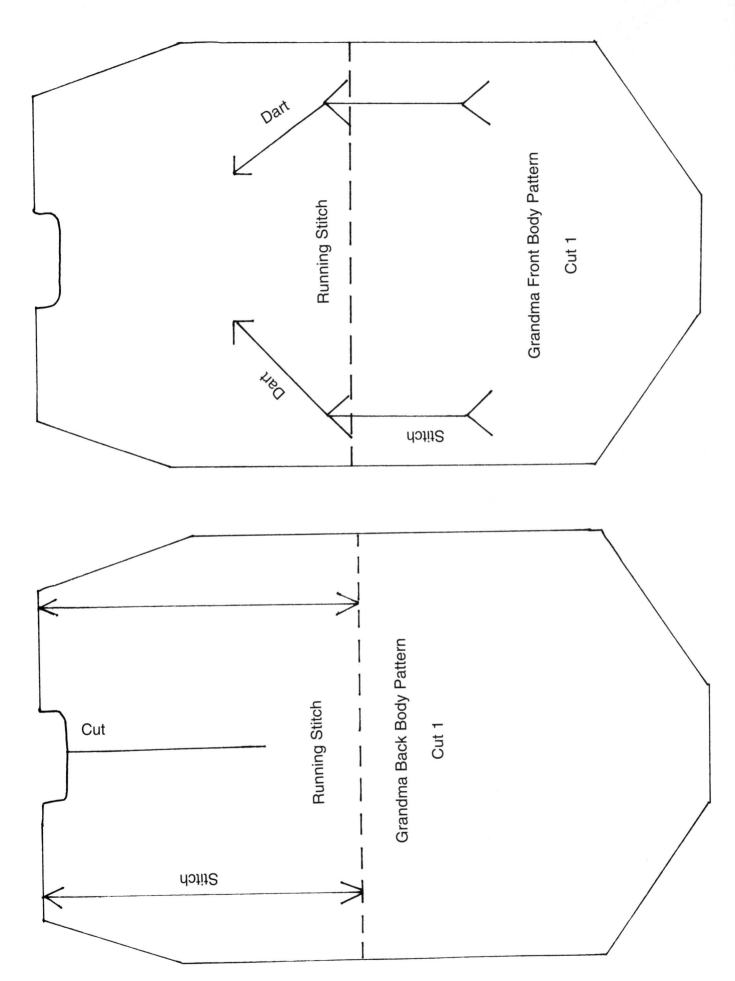

Dart

Running Stitch

Grandma Front Body Pattern

Cut 1

Stitch

Running Stitch

Cut

Grandma Back Body Pattern

Cut 1

Stitch

72

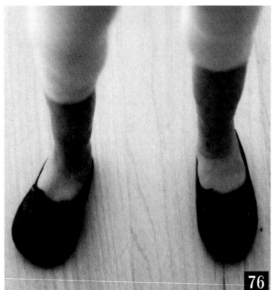
76

77

will allow you to sculpt the arms and legs and thin out whatever you feel is too thick.

Assembling the Armature

65. Using the *Adult Figure Sketch* as a guide, match the leg armature to the drawing. Let the shoes fall below the last line.

66. Once the legs are in place, place the arms where they should fall using the sketch as a guide. Twist the leg wires around the torso wire armature and secure with pliers. Do the same with the arms.

67. Wrap the wire with masking tape. This will soften and help pad the armature for stuffing.

Stuffing the Body

68. Stuff the arms and legs with polyester batting. Use a thin dowel stick or pencil to firmly and evenly stuff all the limbs. Wrap a strip of quilt batting around the torso armature to flesh it out a little. This will aid in maiking the body pattern.

Torso Pattern

69. Place a piece of tracing paper or wax paper over the *Adult Figure Sketch* and draw the body from the top of the shoulders to just below the hips. Remove the paper from the sketch and cut it out.

70. Transfer this pattern to graph paper and add 1/4 inch on all sides for seam allowances. Cut out the pattern and mark it (see *Grandma Body Pattern-page 35*). Transfer the pattern to the muslin and cut out two pieces; one for the front and one for the back.

71. Sew the shoulder and the side seams leaving 1/4 inch seam allowances. Turn the pattern to the right side and at the center of neck edge, on one pattern piece only, cut a line about 1-1/2 inches down. This will be the back of the pattern. The opening that is remaining will allow you to get the pattern over the doll.

72. Pull the muslin pattern over the doll and use the leg, arm, and neck openings to stuff the torso part of the doll. Hand sew around the leg and arm openings. Around the ridge, sew the back and neck closed.

73. Start defining the body. Gather the waist with a running stitch.

74. Make a diagonal dart at the bustline. Use a pencil to draw a diagonal line from the side of the body, starting below the arm, to about 1/2 inch up the front of the body. Make a dart and sew.

75. In the back, draw a line from the waist up to the armhole. Hand sew a dart.

Painting

76. Using acrylic paint, start painting the shoes with a solid neutral

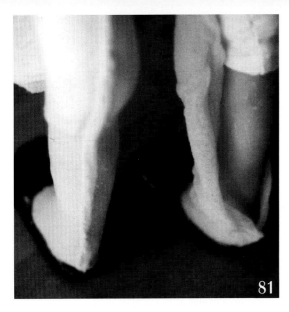

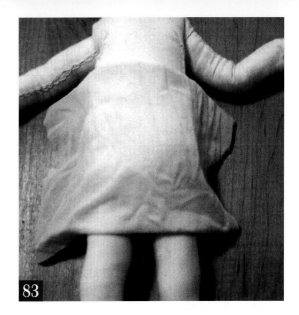

color like cordovan or dark maroon. For the top and bottom of the sole, mix the color you chose with black. Mix antique gold and black together to shade the top of the shoe around the bumps where the big and little toes are. Let them dry. End with a matte finish.

77. Mix water and brown paint until the color is diluted. Brush on paint around the crevices and wrinkles all over the doll's face and hands. Take off the excess paint with your fingers. This will give a shaded effect and bring out the crevices and wrinkles on the doll's face and hands.

78. Mix 3/4 dark maroon with a dab of red and white for the lip stick and nail polish. Apply with a very thin brush. Let the paint dry and end with a matte finish.

Stockings

79. For the stockings, use an old pair of ivory opaque pantyhose. Cut a 6 inch length of stocking in half length-wise.

80. Use a toothpick to apply a clear-drying glue between the slipper and the foot groove. Tuck pantyhose into the grove with the toothpick and making sure the edges of the stocking do not show. When bringing the stockings around to the back, leave just enough stocking to be able to sew a seam. Trim the excess stocking and let them dry.

81. With invisible thread, sew the stocking seam. Hold and fold the stocking inward as you go up the leg. Keep sewing until you reach the top of the leg. Do the same for the other leg.

82. With the thicker panty part of the hose, cut out a square about 6x7 inches.

83. Place the material over the front of the doll and fold the top and bottom edge under for the waist and leg hems.

84. Sew around each leg, the crotch, up the back seam of doll body and around the waist to make the panties.

Making the sleeves of the dress pattern

85. Take a piece of wax paper and wrap it around the arm. Mark the wrist and the top of the arm at the shoulder. Pin the wax paper, adding about 1/4 inch for the seam allowance.

86. Slide the wax paper off of arm. Add 1 inch to the top of the marked line. Draw a line from the wrist marking to the shoulder marking. Cut it out.

87. Transfer the wax paper pattern to graph paper and mark it (see *Grandma Sleeve Pattern—page 38*).

Making the dress pattern

88. Place wax paper on top of the doll and pin it in place. Using a pencil or a sharp tool, loosely trace around the doll's body using the side and shoulder seams of the muslin as a guide. Do not trace too closely to the body. Mark the bottom of the wax paper where the muslin and the leg meet.

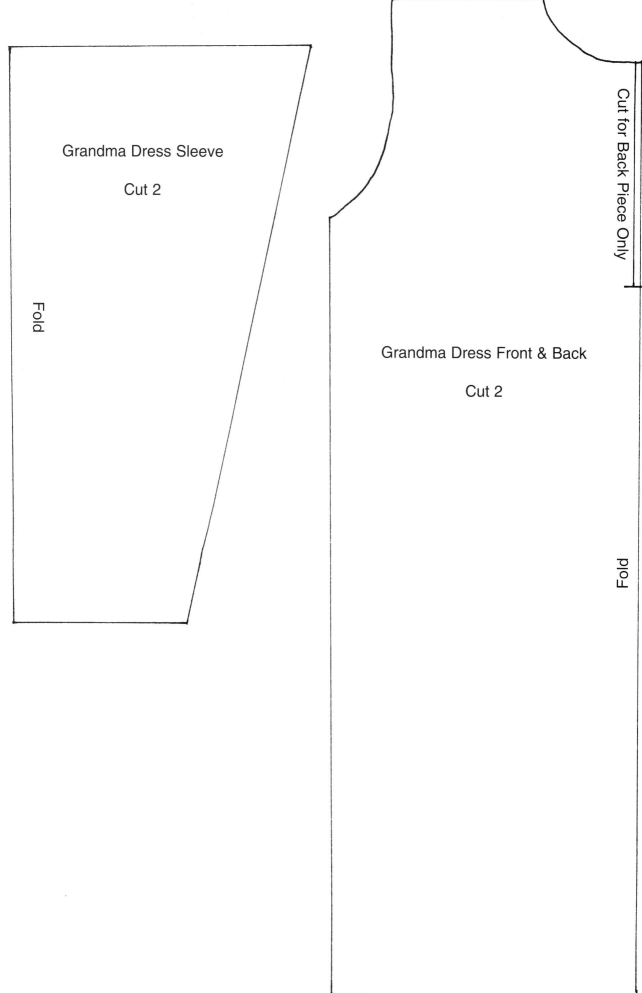

Grandma Dress Sleeve

Cut 2

Fold

Grandma Dress Front & Back

Cut 2

Cut for Back Piece Only

Fold

89. Unpin the wax paper and take it off the doll. Cut out the sketch.

90. Fold the wax paper in half and transfer the pattern onto graph paper (see *Grandma Dress Pattern—page 38*). Define the arm holes and neck edges adding 3/4 inch to all sides. Mark pattern "front" and "back." On the fold side of the pattern, draw a straight vertical line down the pattern about 1-1/2 inches. Mark it as "back only cut." This will be the opening that will allow the dress to slip on the doll.

91. Pin the sleeve and dress graph paper patterns on the material. Cut out one front and one back pattern and two sleeves. A printed material such as calico will do nicely for this dress. Remember to use a small print that stays in scale with the doll.

92. With the right sides together, fold the sleeve in half and sew. Turn the sleeves to the right side. Sew the side seams of the dress up to the armhole. Then, sew the shoulder seams of the dress.

Inserting sleeves

93. The dress is still with the wrong side out. Slide the right side of the sewn sleeve into the armhole (right sides are together), match the seams at underarms, and pin. With pins, gather the extra material on top of the sleeve. Hand sew (only a few stitches) with a running stitch along the very top of the sleeve to pull together to form the cap. Hand sew the sleeves to the dress. Turn right side out and press.

94. Hem the dress to the muslin/leg line. Put the dress on the doll. With a running stitch, gather and sew the dress at the wrist and neck. Sew up the back neck opening.

95. Choose a small lace trimming for the neck and wrist. Hem and sew in place.

Apron

96. Cut a piece of white material (muslin weight is fine) about 6-1/2 x 5 inches for the bottom square. Cut a second square of material about 4-1/2 inches for the upper part. For apron strings, cut out two thin strips of material that are long enough to tie in the back (about twice the width of the larger square). You may also chose to use lace for the apron strings instead of material. Fold over and hem all the sides of the large square. Hem three sides of the smaller square. Pin the hemmed edge of the large square to the raw edge of the smaller square. Make sure that the smaller square is centered on the larger square so the extra material on the larger square's sides will be the same. Sew together. Sew the apron strings to the side edges of the larger square. Cut two small pieces of lace for pockets and hem them at the sides and bottom. Attach them, on a diagonal, to the front of the large part of the apron. Put the apron on the doll and tie in the back.

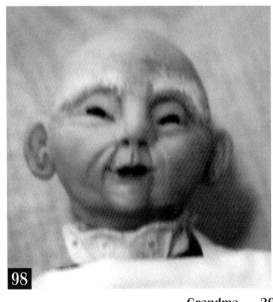

100

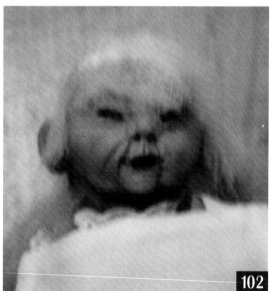

102

103

Eyebrows

97. Use the same color of mohair or sheep's wool as you will use for the doll wig. Cut a thin strip of hair from the material for eyebrows.

98. Use a clear-drying glue and a toothpick to outline the brow line on the doll. With a pair of tweezers, apply bits of the mohair or sheep's wool to the brow. Let them dry and then trim with a small manicuring scissors.

Eyelashes

99. If you are using sheep's wool, pick out the coarser strands from the wool you will be using for the wig. If you are using mohair and you find it too difficult to pick out individual strands, you may also use false eyelashes which you can purchase from a store or a doll supplier.

100. Using scissors, cut strands for eyelashes. With tweezers, dip one end of the lash in the clear-drying glue. Glue each individual lash to the top of the eyelids. Try to space them evenly. Do the same for the lower lids. Let them dry and then trim with a small manicuring scissors.

Wig

101. To make the wig, use white mohair or white/grayish sheep's wool. You may want to mix the two for a nice blend of graying white hair. Use a strip of hair about 7 or 8 inches in length. Spread this out like a fan. Stitch across the hair with the appropriate color thread.

102. With clear-drying glue, glue thin wisps of hair around face and neck line of doll. Let dry.

103. With a hot glue gun, outline the perimeter of the head. You may want to work a section at a time because the hot glue dries very quickly. Start at the center of the head and work around folding the stitched side of wig under as you go. The hair will be hanging down when you have finished.

104. Gather up the hair and twist the strands at the top of the head to form a bun. Don't pull too tightly because a "Gibson" effect will soften the doll's features. You may need to try this a few times before you get it to look right.

105. Make a bow out of the black seam binding or a thin strip of black velvet trim. Place at the center back of the bun and secure it with a hot glue gun.

Jewelry

106. Take a piece of a very thin chain and attach a tiny piece of jewelry to it. A small charm or a piece of an earring will work well. Use jewelry glue to secure a pearl bead to the end of it and let it dry. With wire cutters, cut a very thin piece of gold wire about 2 inches long. String a pearl bead on the wire. Twist and secure with pliers.

107. Put the necklace on the doll to determine the length you want it. Cut excessive chain with a wire cutters. While the necklace is on the doll, try to attach it in the back with pliers. If the chain is too thin, you may want to use epoxy glue to hold the two pieces together.

108. String thin gold wire through the earring openings in the ears. Position a tiny pearl bead on the wire and let the wire drop a tiny bit from ear. Bend wire up to the back of the ear. Secure it in place with pliers.

Glasses

109. Use thin gold wire to make the frames of the glasses. Leave a section of straight wire for the arm of the glasses. Start making the body of the eyeglasses by wrapping a strand of wire around a pencil and tying it.

110. Make another circle with the pencil a little way down the wire strand. Leave enough wire for the other arm of the glasses and cut with wire cutters.

111. Place the glasses on the doll's face and adjust them over the bridge of the doll's nose by bending the wire.

112. Using a flat piece of thin plastic, place the frames of the glasses on the plastic and trace around the circles of the frames with a pencil or sharp tool. Cut out the circles with scissors. Use clear-drying glue to glue around the circles of the eye glasses. Place the plastic circles on the frames and dry.

113. Put the glasses back on the doll and reshape the arms of the frames to fit the doll's head. Wrap the arms around the back of the ear and trim excess wire with wire cutters.

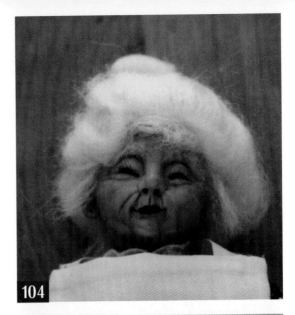

104

105

Cane

114. Roll out a thin cylinder of clay for a cane. Elongate it by rolling it with your fingers. Bend the clay on one end for a handle.

115. Position the doll by bending her into a frail position. Bend her legs a little, and curve her body by having her bottom stick out slightly in the back. Make sure she balances on a flat surface. Measure the cane against the positioned body and cut off any excess length.

116. Bake the cane on a foil covered baking pan in a 275 degree oven. Watch every 10 minutes. When done, let cool on cooling rack.

117. Paint the cane with brown acrylic. Shade using brush strokes up and down the cane with a mixture of brown and black paint. Let the cane dry and end with a matte finish.

Finishing

118. Use a Q-tip to dab a bit of blush on the doll's cheeks, chin and the outside of the hands. ■

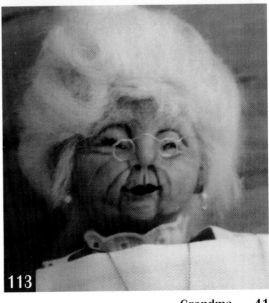

113

For this third project, we will elaborate on what we have learned so far. You'll refine the doll's body including toes, exaggerated fingernails and the continuation of the neck down to the breast plate. The finish on this doll is wax and will be applied after the entire doll body is painted.

Beginning the Body

1. Cut six strands of wire about 10 inches long for the legs, arms, head and torso. Cut two strands of wire about 12 inches long for the torso armature.

Beginning the Head

2. Make a small ball out of foil and run a 10 inch strand of wire through it. Extend a little of the wire over the top of the foil (see *Clown—Beginning the Head* #2). With pliers, bend the top of the wire to make a hook and push it back down into the foil to bury and secure it.
3. On the side of the foil that will be the back of the head, make an indentation by pushing the back of the foil up with your thumbs to form the base of the head.
4. Make four ovals of clay about 2 inches long. Place them on all sides of the foil ball. Smooth the clay over the foil to form head. Leave the indentation at the back of the head; this forms the jaw line.

Sculpting the Face

5. Using an X-acto® knife, divide the face in half by drawing a light vertical line down the center (see *Clown—Sculpting the Face* #6). About halfway down the face, draw a horizontal line for the eyes. Divide that distance with the bottom of the face (chin) and draw a horizontal line for the nose. Divide the nose line and the chin by another horizontal line which forms the mouth.
6. Using your thumbs, depress the clay along the horizontal eye line for the eye sockets. Leave a space for the nose bone in between.
7. Using the blunt tool, make a deep puncture in each eye socket for the eyes. I have used glass, 10mm green eyes. Insert the eyes in the holes making sure both eyes are focused in the same direction and looking straight ahead.
8. Roll out four pieces of clay for the upper and lower lids. Make the upper lids a little bigger than the lower lids to show more of the top eyelid. With the mirror, examine your upper and lower lids when you are looking straight ahead. Notice the position of the eyeball in relation to the rest of the eye. Using a blunt tool, blend the upper lids into eye sockets being careful not to touch the brow bone. Place the lower lids on the eyes and blend them into the face.

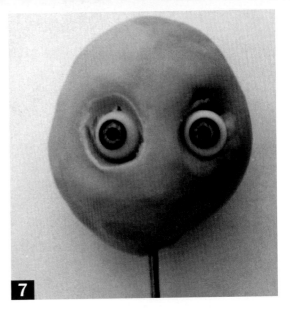

7

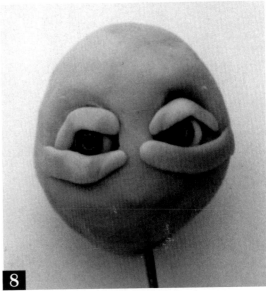

8

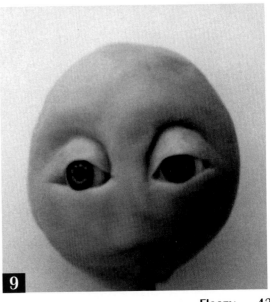

9

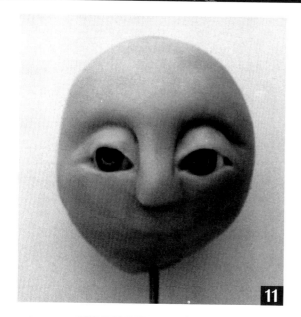

9. Blend the eyes at the inner and outer corners and above the brow bone. We are looking for seductive, almond shaped eyes for the Floozy.

10. Start building the forehead by placing a thin strip of clay horizontally above the eyebrows. Round out the area around the temples with your fingers. Place a thin strip of clay vertically down from the forehead for the bridge of the nose.

11. Use a blunt tool to blend these pieces together. Keep the emphasis on the eyebrow bone as you work to define that portion of the face. Use the blunt tool to end the nose about at the center of where the cheeks will be.

12. Start shaping the rest of the face. Add ovals of clay to the tip of the nose, cheeks, and the area between the lower nose and the upper lip. Use a larger strip of clay for the chin and a small piece for the protruding part of the chin.

13. Blend all of these pieces together with the blunt tool and then smooth them with your fingers. Shape the nose with the blunt tool. Make two holes for the nostrils and then go back into each hole with the blunt tool and round out the inside of the nostril. Use the blunt tool to make a slight indentation between the nostrils and the base of the nose for the septum.

14. Make a smiling mouth line with the X-acto® knife. Again, flesh out the cheeks with ovals of clay. Add ovals to upper area between the nose and mouth and the protruding part of chin.

15. Blend these pieces together with a blunt tool and then smooth them with your fingers. Shape the lower top area of the skin, between the nose and the mouth, by adding two small cylinders of clay below the nostrils. Blend them with the blunt tool. Add a thin cylinder of clay for the lower lip. Then, add another cylinder, for roundness, on either side of the chin. Blend all of these pieces with the blunt tool and then smooth with your fingers.

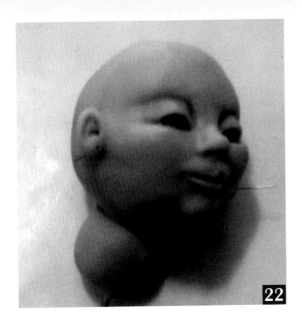
22

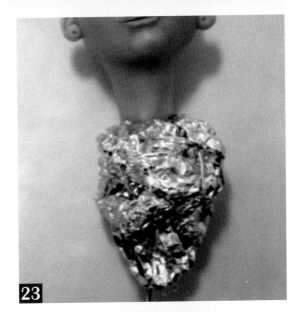
23

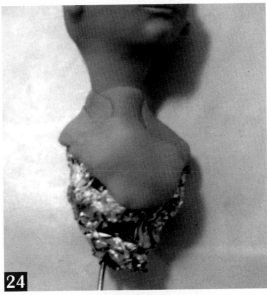
24

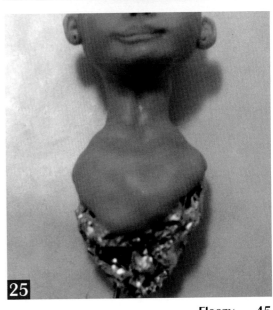
25

Ears and Neck

16. Take a good look at someone's ear. When you are sculpting, have a mirror ready to glance at your own ear as you go along. The ear is placed between the eyebrow and the end of the nose at the side of the head (see *Clown—Ears and Neck #19-22*). Using the X-acto® knife, draw a light vertical line between these two points.

17. Make two small ovals of clay which are the length of the lines. Put the ovals up to the line and turn the head from side to side to make sure of the placement. If the ears are down too far or up too high, they will draw unwanted attention to that area of the head. Secure and smooth the ear with the blunt tool.

18. With the blunt tool in center of ear, make a very small hole that resembles a half moon. Add a tiny round piece of clay to form the protective lobe in the front of the center hole.

19. Use the blunt tool to make the rim around the outer edge of the ear. Draw a half moon from the upper earhole to the bottom where the lobe will be placed. Between the earhole and the outer edge of ear line, make another half moon indentation with the blunt tool. Make a small oval pad for the ear lobe and attach it with the blunt tool.

20. Finish the ear by turning the head to the side. Add a thin vertical clay strip to the back between the head and the ear and blend.

21. Make a hole for the earrings by driving a thin piece of floral wire through the lobe.

22. To create a neck, add a strip of clay around the wire and attach it to the bottom of the face. With the blunt tool, blend it into the back of the head, the jaw and the chin line. Add as many strips of clay as you need and keep blending until you create a neck that suits the head. Too thin or too fat a neck will distort the doll.

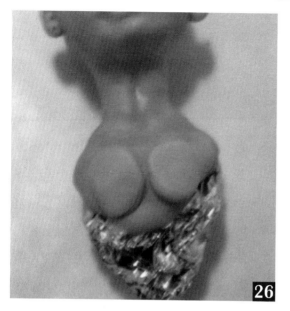

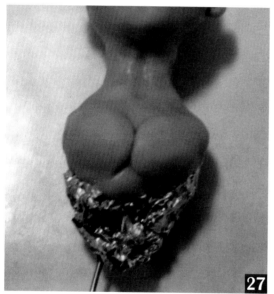

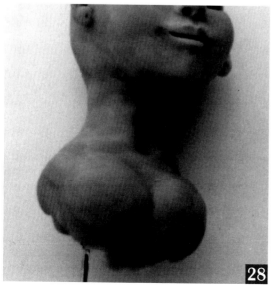

Bust

23. Mold an oval from a crinkled piece of foil. Put it through the bottom of the head wire and bring it up until it touches the neck. This is the base for the breast plate.
24. Roll out a flat piece of clay and wrap it around the foil. Blend it with the blunt tool and then smooth it with your fingers.
25. Shape the neck. Look at your own neck in the mirror. With the blunt tool, make a slight indentation down the lower center of the neck to separate the two vertical neck bones. With the rounded end of the blunt tool, make a small round indentation at the base of the neck. With the blunt tool, separate the collar bones on each side of this round indentation. You may need to add clay when working on each part of the neck if there isn't enough to mold with.
26. Make two ovals for the breasts. Blend with the blunt tool and smooth with your fingers.
27. Define the cleavage with the sharp tool.
28. Bake at 275 degrees on a foil covered baking pan. Check the oven after 15 minutes and every 10 minutes thereafter. When done, let cool on cooling rack. When the breast plate is cold, remove the foil from it.

Hands

29. To measure for the size of the hands, put the doll's head on a piece of paper. Draw two horizontal lines on the paper, one next to the middle of the forehead and another next to the chin. Remove the head from the paper.
30. Starting with the middle finger, roll out a thin piece of clay and place it on the diagram between the lines (see *Clown—Hands* #28). Roll three other pieces of clay of similar size. Look at your own fingers and determine the different lengths. With the X-acto knife, cut down fingers according to size. Leave the middle finger where it is on the diagram. Take a tiny bit of clay off the index finger because that is the next longest. The ring finger is shorter than the middle finger and index finger. The pinkie finger is between the center and the top of the ring finger.
31. Make a small circle of clay for the back of the hand. Put the small circle of clay over one-quarter of the bottom of the shaped fingers to create the outer part of the hand.
32. Take a 10 inch strand of wire and cover 1/4 of the wire with a small cylinder of clay to form the forearm (see *Clown—Hands* #30). Make a paddle on the end of the wire for the palm of the hand.
33. Put the palm and back of hand (step #31) together (see *Clown—Hands* #30). Blend with the blunt tool and smooth with your fingers.
34. Flesh out fingers by placing thin strips of clay over fingers. Blend with the blunt tool until they look like real fingers. Turn hand frequently, working to flesh out palm side as well.

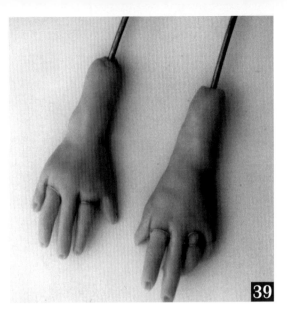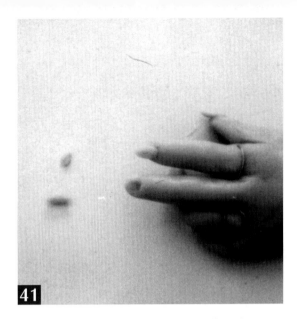

35. Roll a very small cylinder of clay for the thumb (see *Clown—Hand*s #33). Look at your own thumb for placement. Attach the thumb on the index finger side of hand. It should be placed lower down on the hand and not too near the index finger. Blend with the blunt tool to secure it.

36. Shape the thumb to look real by bending it out from the hand slightly. Add a ridge at the bottom of the forearm for when you will attach the muslin arm pattern. Put the hand next to the head again to make sure of the correct proportion.
Make the other hand the same way, except reverse the fingers. When you are rolling out the fingers and placing them, have the other sculpted hand near you so you can be sure you are making the opposite hand.

37. When you have finished the other hand, make sure they are a matching pair in size and shape.

Rings

38. On the left hand, pry the pinkie, ring finger and index finger apart. Do the same on the other hand for the ring and index finger. Use a small piece of thin gold trim or wire and wrap the wire around each finger you have selected for a ring. I have chosen to make four rings, one on each index and ring finger. Twist the wire on the inside of the fingers to secure them and clip the excess with wire cutters or scissors. With the blunt tool, tuck the wire into the clay skin and cover. Gently move the fingers back into position.

Positioning fingers

39. I have left a space between the index and middle finger of the left hand because I intend to have this doll hold a cigarette. I have bent the ring and pinkie finger slightly back. The right hand is just relaxed.

40. Use the sharp pointed tool for the nails. Starting at the tip of the finger, draw a nail. Go back around the sides and with the X-acto® knife, go in and dig a little of the nail out.

Long nails

41. Roll out tiny pieces of clay that are shaped like rods with round points at each end. Using the flatter part of a tool, pick up the pieces and place them in the nail beds. Tuck in and secure with the sharp pointed tool. Do not make the nails too long for they may break as you work.

42. Use the X-acto® knife to carve the lines for the knuckles. Start in the middle of the finger and draw a short line. Keep adding lines around the center of the finger until you have created a real looking knuckle.
Look at the lines and creases on the back of your hands and recreate them on the doll's hand.

43. Sign the palm of the doll's hand or you may wish to wait and sign the bottom of the shoe. With the sharp tool, carve in the palm, your initials, an abbreviated date, and a small copyright symbol ©.

44. With the blunt tool, make round indentations around the upper forearm to form ridges to attach muslin arm pattern.

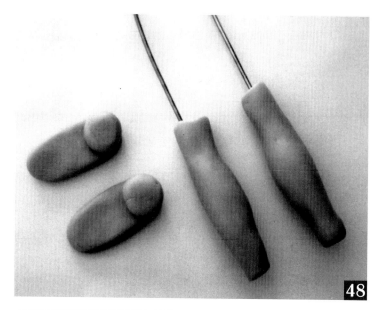

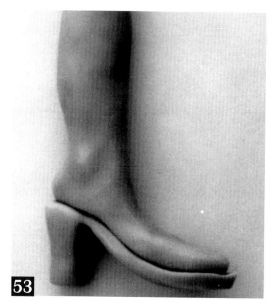

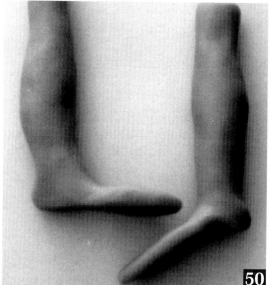

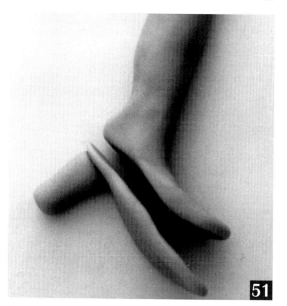

45. Bake the hands in the oven on a foil covered pan at 275 degrees. Watch the hands every 10 minutes because they are thin and may cook quickly. When done, place on a cooling rack.

Legs and Sandals

46. Roll out two cylinders of clay for the lower half of the leg (see *Clown—Legs and Shoes* #42). Make stumps thick enough to provide stability. They will be helping to hold the weight of the entire doll so they can not be too thin. Use two, 10 inch strands of wire and put them through the middle of the cylinder. Do not go all the way through to the bottom or it will continue to protrude through the foot.

47. Using your own lower leg as a guide, start sculpting the calf and ankle. Pare off excess clay with the X-acto® knife. Use your fingers as you go along to smooth the clay.

48. Start shaping the foot. Roll out a flat piece of clay about 1/4 inch thick. With the X-acto® knife, cut out two narrow ovals. Put these ovals up to the head of the doll and measure from the middle of the forehead to the chin. These ovals are smaller than the general shoe measurement because they are the feet.

49. Measuring for the sandals is the next step. Roll two small ovals for the ankles. These pieces of clay will connect the lower leg to the foot. Place these small ovals on the heel part of the foot.

50. Blend the legs into the feet. Narrow the back of the clay for a heel with your fingers.

51. Arch the foot. Look at your own foot and pose it as if it was going to slide into a high heel shoe.

52. Start shaping the shoe. Roll out two more narrow ovals a little larger than the feet. Measure these to the head. They should measure from the top of the head to the chin. These will be the sole of the sandals. Make a small cylinder for the heel of the sandal.

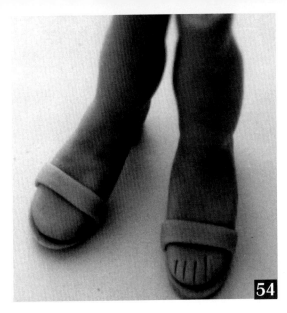

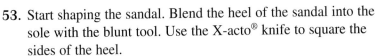

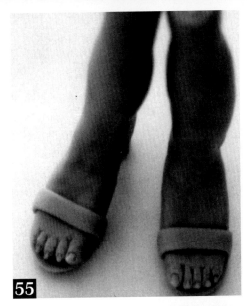

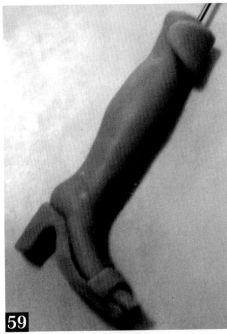

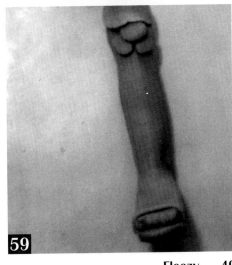

53. Start shaping the sandal. Blend the heel of the sandal into the sole with the blunt tool. Use the X-acto® knife to square the sides of the heel.

54. Roll out two thin strips of clay for the top of the sandals and attach them on each side with the blunt tool. Use the X-acto® knife to cut lines for toes. Space out the lines so that there is extra space where the big toe will go on each foot.

55. Use the blunt tool to shape each individual toe. Round them as you go. With a sharp pointed tool, go back and redraw the lines between each toe and join them into the foot with creases that are shaped like little "v's".

56. Use the sharp pointed tool for the nails. Starting at the tip of the toe, draw a nail. Outline the sides again with the X-acto® knife, then dig a little of the nail out. Roll out tiny pieces of clay rods. Using the flatter part of a tool, pick up the pieces and place them in the nail beds. Tuck in and secure with the sharp pointed tool. With the blunt tool, go back and slightly square off nail edges. Make sure toes are lifted a little from shoe to create a real look.

57. Add a small oval of clay at the top of the shaped leg for the knee. Blend this piece into the front of the leg with the blunt tool. Smooth with your fingers.

58. Start shaping the upper portion of the leg by adding pieces of clay on each side of knee. Look in the mirror at your own leg and notice how the area above the knee is fuller. Blend with the blunt tool and smooth with your fingers.

59. Start detailing the kneecap and the rest of the knee. Roll out two small ovals of clay for the flesh on each side of the kneecap. Make another small oval for the knee cap in the center of the ovals. Roll out a small rectangle of clay for the upper area above the knee. Blend these pieces together one at a time to keep them defined.

60. With the blunt tool, draw a ring around the upper part of the

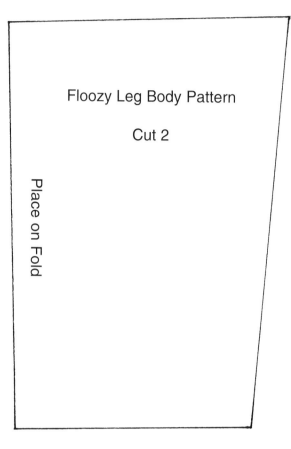

Floozy Arm Body Pattern

Cut 2

Place on Fold

Floozy Leg Body Pattern

Cut 2

Place on Fold

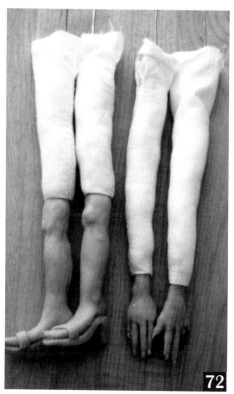

leg for the ridge that will connect the upper leg with muslin leg pattern.

61. Bake legs and sandals in a 275 degree oven on a foil covered baking pan. Check pieces after 15 minutes and every 10 minutes thereafter. These will take a little longer to bake because they are thicker. When done, let cool on cooling rack.

Armature:

Refer to Adult Figure Sketch. This is the guide you will be working from for measuring armature.

62. Take two, 12 inch wire strands and twist them together for the torso (see *Clown—Armature #51*).

63. Attach the head to the torso by twisting the head wire to the torso armature. To determine the height of the doll, take the head measurement from the chin to the forehead and multiply by 8. We are using 8 because proportionally, an average adult doll will stand 7-1/2 to 8 heads high for correct scaling of the body parts. For example, my doll's head measures 2 inches. Multiplying by 8 yields 16. Thus, 16 inches will be the height of the doll.

Arm and Leg Pattern

All of the pattern pieces are marked and ready for use. Before using these pattern pieces, always check them against your

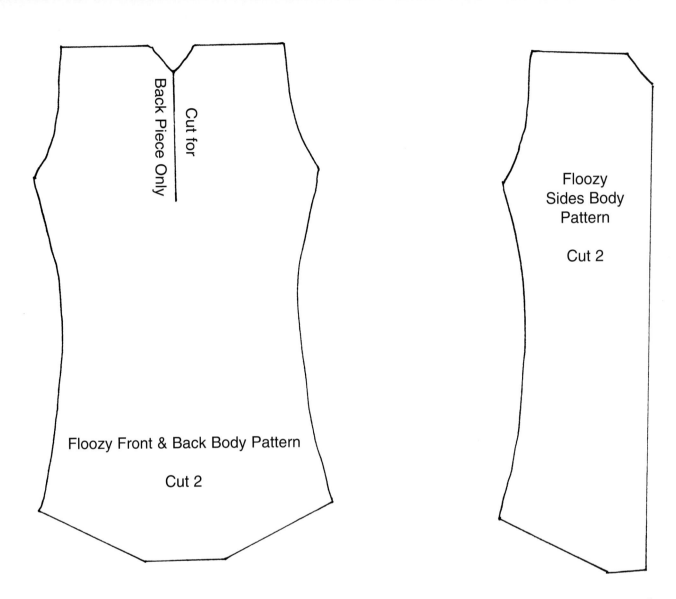

Back Piece Only

Cut for

Floozy
Sides Body
Pattern

Cut 2

Floozy Front & Back Body Pattern

Cut 2

doll. Since you are making an original doll, your measurements may not be the same as mine so you may have to alter these patterns slightly to fit your own doll.

64. Cut out four 8x5 inch pieces of muslin for the arms and legs. The width and length of the muslin are approximate at this point. Place the forearm part of the armature on the edge of the muslin. Place the lower leg armature close to the muslin edge. Do this for all four pieces of armature.

65. Fold the muslin over the armature.

66. Go back to the sketch and measure the arm on the figure from the top of the shoulder to the hand. It measures about 6 inches. You will need extra length for sewing and attaching the armature to the torso. A measurement of about 7-1/4 inches will give you enough length to work with. It is better to shorten the pattern than to have to start over. This measurement will be fine for the legs also.

67. Measure the width of the muslin by leaving about 1/2 inch extra muslin for sewing the seams on the pattern. Put the ruler on the wrist about 1/4 inch away from the clay and mark it with a dot. Draw a diagonal line from that point to the top edge of the muslin. This will create a thinner section for the forearm and a wider section as you go up the arm. The leg pattern pieces can be straighter and wider because the upper leg is heavier and the added weight will help the finished doll stand alone.

68. Cut the muslin arm pattern to size. Before sewing these pieces, put the arm and leg muslin on a piece of cardboard and trace it. Mark it and cut it out for future use. With a sewing machine, stitch all four pieces leaving

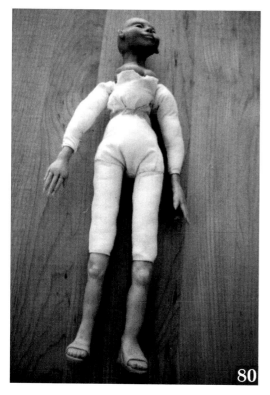

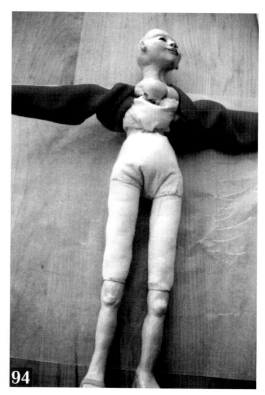

1/4 inch seam allowance (see *Floozy Arm and Leg Body Pattern—page 50*).

Attaching Muslin to Arm and Leg Armature

69. Attach the muslin pattern to the arms and legs by pulling the pieces over each of the arms and legs so that the wrong side of the muslin is facing out (see *Clown—Attaching Muslin to Arm and Leg Armature #60*). Pull the material down just below the ridges. Make sure the seams of the muslin are in the back of the legs and the palm side of the hands.

70. Fill the ridges of the armature with glue (see *Clown—Attaching Muslin to Arm and Leg Armature #60*). Pull the muslin up over the glued ridges. Since the muslin will not fit tightly over the wrist ridges, pull the material on each side of the seam at the back and overlap like a dart. Make sure excess material is facing toward the center of seam. Secure the material with a small piece of thin wire (floral wire works well).

71. Let pieces dry

72. When the glue has dried, pull the muslin up to form the cloth part of the arms and legs.

Assembling the Armature:

73. Using the *Adult Figure Sketch* as a guide, match the leg armature to the drawing. Let the shoes fall below the last line. Twist the leg wires around the torso wire armature and secure the wire with pliers. Once the legs are in place, put the doll back on the figure and put the arms where they should fall using the sketch as a guide. Twist the arm wires around the top of the torso wire armature and secure with pliers.

Stuffing the Body:

74. Wrap the wire with masking tape. This will soften and help pad the armature for stuffing.

75. Stuff the arms and legs with polyester batting. Use a thin dowel stick or pencil to firmly and evenly stuff all limbs. Wrap a strip of quilt batting around the torso armature to flesh it out a little to aid in making the body pattern.

Torso Pattern:

76. Place tracing paper or wax paper over the *Adult Figure Sketch* and draw the body from the top of the shoulders to just below the hips. Remove it from the sketch and cut it out.

77. Transfer this pattern to the graph paper and add 1/4 inch on all sides for a seam allowance (see *Floozy Body and Side Patterns—page 51*). Cut out the pattern and mark it on the front and back. Draw a straight line about 1-1/2 inches long down the center of this pattern marking it "back only." This will be the opening to get the pattern over the doll's body. Fold pattern in half and trace just half of pattern. Mark it "side of body pattern."

78. Transfer pattern to muslin and cut the pattern twice for the front and back. Sew sides to back and then sides to front leaving 1/4 inch seam allowances. Sew crotch front to back. Leave the top open.

79. Pull the muslin pattern over doll.

80. Use the leg, arm, and neck openings to stuff the torso part of the doll. Stuff bottom half of doll body heavily. Lightly stuff from the waist up. Hand sew around leg openings. Sew around the armhole openings to the breast plate. Leave the neck open.

81. Shape the body by taking two tucks at the waistline in front and back for indentation. Stuff a little bit below the breast plate. Leave the muslin around the breast plate open.

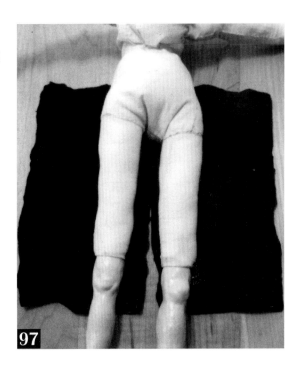

Painting:

82. Using acrylic paint, mix fleshtone and a little bit of brown until you get a creamy look. Apply to the face, bust, hands, legs and feet. Be careful not to get the paint in the doll's eyes or on her rings and sandals. Let first coat dry and then apply another coat.

83. Later, when you have decided on the gown material, paint the doll's features. For the lipstick, fingernails and toe nails, mix colors to complement the doll's gown. For this doll, I used a mixture of red, dark pink, and maroon with a dab of white. Apply with a thin brush.

84. Mix a tiny bit of red and white to form a pale pink blush color. Apply that very softly with a thicker bristled brush to the cheeks.

85. Use black for eyeliner. Line the entire top lid, but only the outer corners of the bottom lids.

86. Use a watery white for the shadow on the eyelids.

87. The entire sandal is painted gold.

88. Let the paint dry thoroughly.

89. Mix fleshtone and brown again only a few shades darker than in #82. Water down the mixture and wash over face, cleavage, hands, legs and feet. Smudge excess paint with fingers. Accentuate wherever there are creases or crevices. Let dry.

90. A matte finish may be applied to everything except lips, finger and toenails which should be finished with a gloss. I have finished this doll in wax. It is a simple process. Use any type of floor wax sold in supermarkets. Apply one coat. Let dry overnight. The finish will be glossy and very pretty. If you would like to experiment and take this step farther, apply the blush

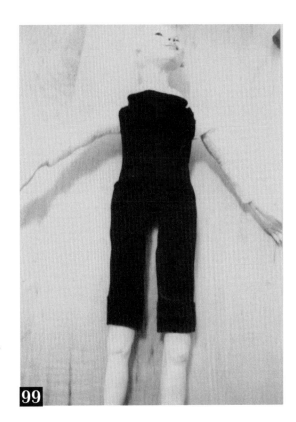

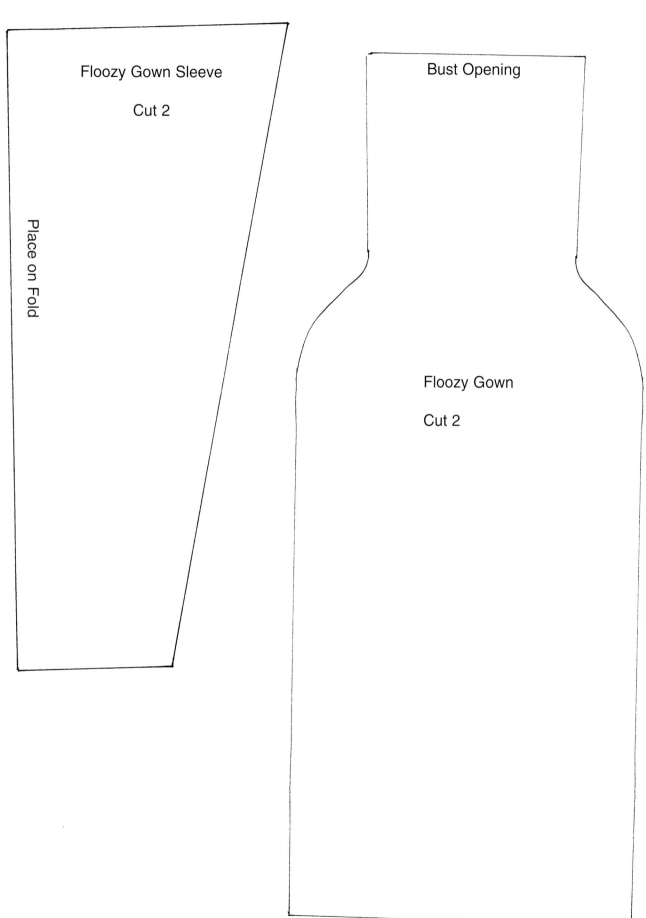

Floozy Gown Sleeve

Cut 2

Place on Fold

Bust Opening

Floozy Gown

Cut 2

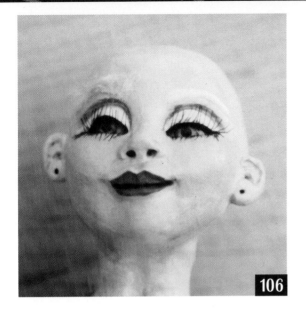

106

107

and more eyeshadow to the doll after the first coat of wax has dried. Reapply the wax for a second coat and let dry overnight.

Sleeves:

91. Take a piece of wax paper and wrap it around the arm. Mark the wrist and the top of the arm at the shoulder. Pin the wax paper leaving about 1/4 inch extra for seam allowance.
92. Slide wax paper off of arm. Add 1 inch to the top marking line. Draw a line from the wrist marking to the shoulder marking. Cut out. Transfer to graph paper (see *Floozy Gown Sleeves—page 54*).
93. Transfer to graph paper. Pin the pattern to the material and cut two sleeves. Double the thickness of the material if it is too see-through or flimsy. Fold sleeves in half on the wrong side and sew.
94. Turn to the right side and slip the sleeves on the doll.

Gown:

95. Place wax paper on top of the doll and pin to hold. Using a pencil or sharp tool, loosely trace around the doll's body coming in at the waist and going up straight just to the bustline. Do not plan for the arms. Mark bottom of wax paper slightly below knee. Unpin the wax paper and take it off the doll.
96. Fold the wax paper in half and transfer the pattern onto graph paper. Once you straighten out one side of the pattern, fold it in half on the graph paper and cut. This will assure both sides are equal. Add 3/4 inch to all sides (see *Floozy Gown pattern—page 54*). Mark pattern "gown cut 2."

Panties:

97. With the heavier top of black pantyhose, cut out a 5 inch square. Place the pantyhose under the lower portion of the doll. Make sure you have enough room to cover the waist plus a bit more. Cut the piece in half up to just below the crotch.
98. Fold the outer sides in and hand sew the inner legs up and the seam in the back.
99. Put the panties on the doll. Stretch the material up and make little holes for the arms. Put each arm through these holes. This forms a body stocking and will help to hold in the breast plate. Sew lace on the bottom of the stocking where the leg and clay meet. Trim the top of the stocking around the breast plate if needed.

Sewing the Gown:

100. Cut out the two front and back gown pattern pieces onto the material. A soft fabric such as a knit or silk-like texture will do nicely.
101. Sew up the side of the dress to the armhole. To leave a slit, sew the other side from the thigh up. Hem the bottom of the dress below the knee.

108

113

102. Hand sew the top of the dress and sleeves together while on the doll. Fold the excess wrist material under like a hem.

103. Sew a flounced trim around the wrists, bustline and hemline to decorate the gown.

Eyelashes:

104. If you choose to make the eyelashes out of mohair, try to pick out the stronger individual strands. If that isn't possible, you may want to try false eyelashes which you can purchase from a store, doll supplier, craft store or catalogue. If using mohair, use tweezers to pick up individual strands and cut them up for eyelashes. With tweezers, dip one end in clear-drying glue and glue each individual lash to the top of the eyelids. Try to space them evenly. Do the same for the lower lids. Because we are trying to achieve a glamorous effect, place the lashes close together. Let dry. Trim with a small manicuring scissors leaving the lashes longer to maintain the effect.

Eyebrows:

105. Using blonde mohair (which will match the doll's wig), cut a thin strip of hair from the mohair for the eye brows. Use clear-drying glue and a toothpick to outline the brow line on the doll.

106. With a pair of tweezers, apply bits of hair to the brow. Let dry and trim with small manicuring scissors.

Jewelry:

107. Pictured here are two earrings and one charm for the necklace. I have used the gold decorative part between each of these beads for the earrings, necklace and part of a ring. Since it is impossible to recreate these bits and pieces of jewelry, use your imagination when seeing a piece. Picture how it will look on the doll and put it against the doll to check for size. Some pieces can be larger depending upon the look you are trying to achieve.

108. Find a thin chain and fasten the necklace charm. Determine the length you want, perhaps just above the cleavage, and cut the excessive chain with a wire cutter. While the necklace is on the doll, try to fasten it in the back with pliers. Pull a tiny piece of chain of one end apart and then reattach it to the other end. If the chain is too thin to reattach, you may want to use epoxy glue to hold the two pieces together.

109. Put each earring on a piece of thin wire and put it through the earring holes. Twist the wire in the back of the earhole with the small pliers to secure.

110. The wrist bracelets and ankle bracelets are attached in the same way as the necklace. The wrist bracelets can be thicker and of a slightly bigger pattern.

111. The rings are just bits of jewelry glued onto the already existing ring bands. Use jewelry glue to secure the

pieces, since it is especially made for bonding pieces of jewelry.

Wig:

112. Choose a shade of mohair that complements your doll's skin coloring and costume. You may want to mix two shades for a nice blend, perhaps accentuating the hairline or the top of the head for a frosted look. I have chosen an ash blonde for this doll. Cut a strip of hair about 8 or 9 inches in length.

113. Fan out the strip of mohair. With a hot glue gun, outline the perimeter of the head. You may want to work a section at a time because the hot glue dries very fast. Start at the base of the head in the back and work around folding the edges under as you go. The hair will be off the forehead when you have finished.

114. Fan out and fluff the hair in the back of the doll's head.

115. Turn the doll around to the front. Choose a piece of decorative trim for the headband which complements the doll's costume. Take one end of the headband and start at the back neckline of the doll and secure it with a dab of hot glue. Bring the headband around the doll's head bringing down a section of the front bang as you go. Fluff up the top of the hair and continue until you reach the other side of the back of the head. You may need to try this a few times before you get it to look right. With a hot glue gun, join the headband together in the back.

116. Bring the hair around the shoulders.

Cigarette and Holder:

117. Use an X-acto® knife to cut a small, thin, rod of wood the length you would like the cigarette. Measure it next to doll to be sure it is not too long or too short.

118. Roll a very thin cylinder of clay and wrap it around one end of the wood rod. Let the clay extend a bit out from the wood and flatten it for the lip holder.

119. Bake in a 275 degree oven on a foil covered baking pan. Because this piece is thin, check after 5 minutes. Let cool on cooling rack.

120. Use white acrylic paint for the cigarette. Let dry. Paint the cigarette holder black. Let dry. End with a matte finish on both.

121. Dip the cigarette end in quick-drying clear glue and then add a few tiny pieces of oregano. Let dry. Use a bit of orange, red, and black acrylic paint on the tip to look as if the cigarette is lit.

Finishing:

122. Pose the doll in a seductive way. Maybe one leg will be placed in front of the other. Move the arms to look alluring as she holds her cigarette. ■

Child

For this doll, we will be using the same dollmaking principals we learned in the first three projects. The major challenge with this doll is the different scale of the doll. Follow the *Child Figure Sketch* for measuring the body parts to scale.

Beginning the Body

1. Cut six strands of wire about 6 inches long for the legs, arms, head and torso. Cut two strands of wire about 8 inches long for the torso armature.

Beginning the Head

2. Make a very small ball out of foil and run a 6 inch strand of wire through it. Extend a little of the wire over the top of the foil. With pliers, bend the top of the wire to make a hook and push it back down into the foil to bury and secure it (see *Clown—Beginning the Body* #2).

3. On the side of the foil that will be the back of the head, make an indentation by pushing the back of the foil up with your thumbs to form the base of the head.

4. Make four ovals of clay about 1-1/2 inches long. Place them on all sides of the foil ball. Smooth clay over foil to form head. Leave the indentation at the back of the head which forms the jaw line.

Sculpting the Face

5. Using an X-acto® knife, divide the face in half by drawing a light vertical line down the center (see *Clown—Sculpting the Face* #6). About halfway down the face, draw a horizontal line for the eyes. Divide that distance with the bottom of the face (chin) and draw a horizontal line for the nose. Divide the nose line and chin by another horizontal line which forms the mouth.

6. Using the blunt tool, make a deep puncture in each eye socket. Leave a space for the nose bone in between. I used 6mm glass, blue eyes. Insert the eyes in the holes. Make sure both eyes are focused in the same direction and are looking straight ahead.

7. Roll out four tiny pieces of clay for the upper and lower lids. With the mirror, look at the way your lids look when you are looking straight ahead. Notice the position of the eyeball in relation to the rest of the eye. Using a blunt tool, blend the upper lids into eye sockets being careful not to touch the brow bone. Place the lower lids on the eyes and blend into face.

8. Start building the forehead by placing a thin strip of clay horizontally above the eyebrows. Round out around the temples with your fingers. Place a thin strip of clay vertically down from the forehead for the bridge of the nose. Use a blunt tool to blend these pieces together. Keep the emphasis on the eye brow bone as you work to define that portion of the face.

9. Start shaping the face with an oval piece of clay that covers the bottom half of face. Blend with the blunt tool and then with your fingers.

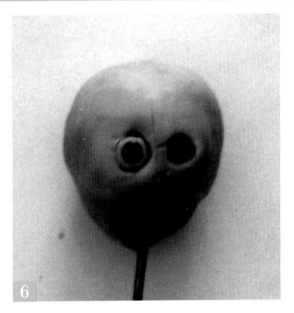

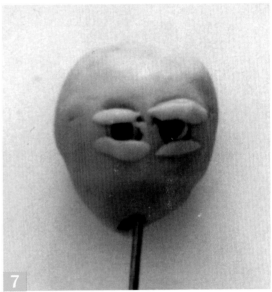

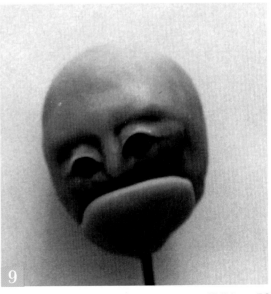

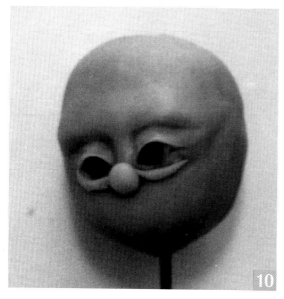

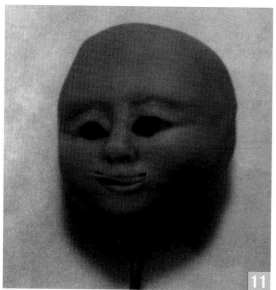

10. Shape the nose by putting a small round ball of clay where the bulb of nose should be. Add thin strips of clay under the eyes and blend with the blunt tool into the sides of the bridge of the nose. With the blunt tool, bring some of the ball of clay up into the upper portion of the bridge of the nose and blend.

11. Draw the smile of the mouth line with the X-acto® knife. Again, flesh out the cheeks with ovals.

12. Add a tiny round circle to the tip of the nose. With a sharp edged tool, make two holes for the nostrils and then go back into each hole with the blunt tool and round out the inside of the nostril. Add a very tiny strip of clay from the tip of the nose to the base, between the nostrils for the septum. Blend with the blunt tool. Add a small circle of clay for the chin.

13. Shape the mouth. Open the mouth with the flat part of the X-acto® knife. Opening the mouth will reshape the bottom half of the face and should bring out the cheeks more. Add two very thin strips of clay for upper and lower lips.

Teeth

14. Insert a tiny strip of clay into the mouth. Secure with a sharp pointed tool. With the X-acto® knife, cut straight vertical lines into the strip to form teeth. You may only be able to cut 3 in this tiny mouth. Leave a large space for a missing tooth in the front. Round out the remaining teeth with the sharp tool.

15. Define the upper lip by using the round end of the blunt tool to make tiny half moons in the center of the lip.

16. With the blunt tool, draw a light line down from the center of the nose to the lips. Also deepen the line forming the cheeks that falls diagonally from the nose to the mouth. With the blunt tool, push in the corners of the mouth to form dimples.

Ears and Neck

17. Take a good look at someone's ear. When you're sculpting, have a mirror ready to glance at your own ear as you go along. The ear is placed between the eyebrow and the end of the nose at the side of the head (see *Clown—Ears and Neck* #18). Using the X-acto® knife, draw a light vertical line between these two points.

18. Make two small ovals of clay the length of the lines. Put the ovals up to the line and turn the head from side to side to make sure of the placement. If the ears are down too far or up too high, they will draw unwanted attention to that area of the head. Attach the ears to the head (see *Clown—Ears and Neck* #19). Secure and blend the ear with the blunt tool.

19. Roll out a strip of clay and wrap it around the wire armature just below the chin for the neck. You may want to hold this part of the neck to sculpt the tiny ear.

20. With the blunt tool in the center of the ear, make a very small hole that resembles a half moon. Add a tiny round piece of clay to form the protective lobe in the front of the center hole.

21. Use the blunt tool to make the rim around the outer edge of the ear. Draw a half moon from the upper earhole to the bot-

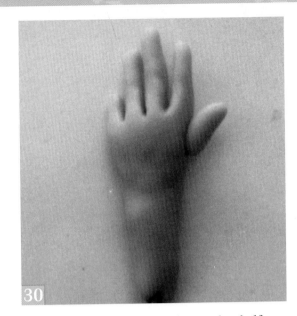

tom where the lobe will be placed. Between the earhole and the outer edge of the ear line, make another half moon indentation with the blunt tool. Make a small oval pad for the ear lobe and attach it with the blunt tool.

22. Finish ears by turning the head to the side. Add a very thin vertical clay strip to the back between the head and the ears. Blend them.

23. Start building up the neck by adding a strip of clay to the already existing strip and blend into the back of the head and jaw line with the blunt tool. Add strips and keep blending until you create a neck that suits the head. Too thin or too fat will distort the doll. With the blunt tool, make a ridge around the lower part of the neck for securing the muslin body pattern.

24. Bake the head in the oven at 275 degrees on a foil covered baking pan. Check clay after 15 minutes and every 10 minutes thereafter until done. Cool on cooling rack.

Hands

25. To measure for the size of the hands, put the head on a piece of paper. Draw two horizontal lines on the paper, one next to the middle of the forehead and another next to the chin. Remove the head from the paper.

26. Starting with the middle finger, roll out a thin piece of clay and place it on the diagram between lines. Roll three other pieces of clay of similar size. Look at your own fingers and determine the different lengths. With an X-acto® knife, cut down the fingers according to size. Leave the middle finger where it is on the diagram. Take a tiny bit of clay off the index finger since that is the next longest. The ring finger is shorter than the middle and index finger. The pinkie finger is between the center and top of the ring finger.

27. Take a 6 inch strand of wire and cover 1/4 of the wire with a small cylinder of clay to form the forearm. Make a paddle on the end of the wire for the palm of the hand.

28. Put a small circle of clay over 1/4 of the bottom of the shaped fingers to create the outer part of the hand. Put the palm and back of hand together. Blend with the blunt tool and smooth with your fingers.

29. Flesh out fingers by placing thin strips of clay over fingers. Blend with blunt tool until they look like real fingers. Flesh out the rest of the hand by building up thin pieces of clay over outer part of hand. Turn hand frequently, working to flesh out palm side as well.

30. Roll a very small cylinder of clay for the thumb. Look at your own thumb for placement. Attach the thumb on the index finger side of hand (see *Clown—Hands* #33). It should be placed lower down on the hand and not too near the index finger. Blend with blunt tool.

31. Make the other hand the same way, except reverse the fingers. When you are rolling out the fingers and placing them, have the other sculpted hand near you so you can be sure you are making the opposite hand. When you have finished the other hand, make sure both are a matching pair in size and shape.

32. Shape thumbs to look real. Add a ridge at the bottom of the forearm for attaching muslin body. Put the hands next to the head again to check the proportions.

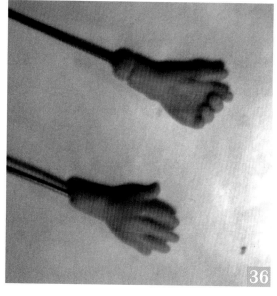

36

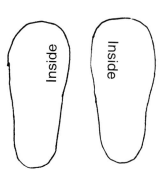

40

Child Shoe Pattern

33. Use your own hands as a guide in determining placement of nails and knuckles. This enlargement of the nails should help you when sculpting (see *Grandma—Hands* #36). Use the sharp pointed tool for the nails. Starting at the tip of the finger, draw a nail. Go back around the sides and indent the nail so it stands out in clay. Go back and lift the tip of the nail a bit for a more rounded effect.

34. Use the X-acto® knife to carve the lines for the knuckles. Start in the middle of the finger and draw a short line and then keep adding lines around the center of the finger until you have created a real looking knuckle. Look at the lines and creases on the back of your hands and recreate them on the inside of the dolls hand.

Positioning fingers

35. I have bent the right fingers slightly so the doll can hold something. The left hand is just relaxed.

36. With blunt tool, make round indentations around the upper wrist to form ridges to attach the muslin arm patern.

37. Sign the palm or you may wish to wait and sign the bottom of the shoe. With the sharp tool, carve your initials, an abbreviated date, and a small copyright symbol ©.

38. Bake the hands in the oven on a foil covered pan at 275 degrees. Watch the hands every 10 minutes because they are thin and may cook quickly. When hands are done, cool on a cooling rack.

Legs and Shoes

39. Put the head on a piece of paper and draw a horizontal line at the top of the forehead and at the chin.

40. Using this measurement as a guide for the shoes, draw a sketch of a shoe between these lines (see *Child Shoe Pattern*). Remember there is an inside and an outside edge to the shoe and the heel is narrower. Mark the inside of the shoe so you will know the left from the right. Cut out this paper sole and trace it to cardboard. Cut out the cardboard sole and place it face down on the cardboard to create the other shoe. Trace, draw, and cut out the other shoe. Mark "inside" on the opposite shoe.

41. Use a rolling pin to roll out a flat piece of clay about 1/4 inch thick. Put the cardboard shoe patterns on the flat piece of clay and trace them lightly with the sharp tool. Take the patterns off the clay and use the X-acto® knife to cut them out. These will be the soles of the shoes.

42. Roll out two cylinders of clay for the lower half of the leg. Make stumps thick enough to provide stability. They will be helping to hold the weight of the entire doll so they can not be too thin. Use two 6 inch strands of wire and put them through the middle of the cylinder. Do not go all the way through to the bottom or it will continue to protrude through the shoe.

43. Using your own lower leg as a guide, start carving calf and ankle. Pare off excess clay with X-acto® knife. Use your fingers as you go along to smooth the clay.

44. Start shaping the shoe. Roll out another piece of flat clay. Trace 3/4 of the front portion of the sole of the shoe with the sharp pointed tool and cut it out with the X-acto® knife. Use four small ovals of clay, two for the big toe and two for the small toes on each shoe. Position them on the tops of the front portion of the shoe. Roll out

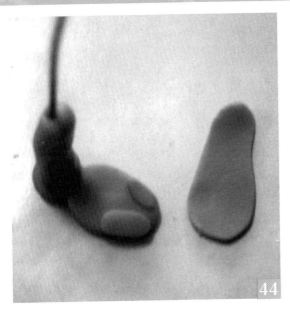

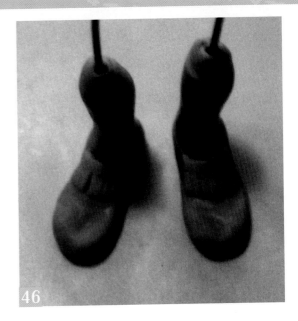

a ball of clay for the ankle and place them over the heel portion of the sole.

45. Blend the lower leg into the ankle. Add clay to ankle to thicken and reinforce if necessary. Blend these pieces together with the blunt tool and then your fingers. Leave the upper shoe defined all around the sole of the shoe as it is the heel part of the shoe. Do the same for the other leg.

Shoe style

46. Clearly define the sole of the shoe from the upper body of the shoe by drawing a light line around the shoe. Leave a deep crevice where the shoe and the leg meet below the ankle. This will be where the tights are glued to the leg.

47. To make fringe for the shoe, roll out a small, flat rectangle of clay. With X-acto® knife, cut evenly spaced vertical lines about 3/4 of the way up the strip. Fit them on the shoe and cut any extra fringe. Blend sides with blunt tool.

48. Make sure shoe and foot are clearly defined. Make ridge at top of lower leg for attaching muslin leg pattern by taking the blunt tool and making a ring around the leg.

49. Bake in oven at 275 degrees on a foil covered baking pan. Check the piece after 15 minutes and every 10 minutes thereafter. When done, let them cool on cooling rack.

Armature

Refer to Child Figure Sketch. This is the guide you will be working from for measuring the armature.

50. Take two 8 inch wire strands and twist them together for the torso (see *Clown—Armature #51*).

51. Attach the head to the torso by twisting the head wire to the torso wire armature and secure with pliers.

52. To determine the height of the doll, take the head measurement from the chin to the forehead and multiply by 7-1/2 or 8. An average doll will stand 7-1/2 to 8 heads high in order to correctly scale all of the body parts. For example, my doll's head measures between 1 and 1-1/8 inches. Multiplying by 8 yields 9 inches which will be the height of the doll. The measuring doesn't have to be that exact, it is just a guide.

Arm and Leg Pattern

All of the pattern pieces are marked and ready for use. Before using these pattern pieces, always check them against your doll. Since you are making an original doll, your measurements may not be the same as mine so you may have to alter these patterns slightly to fit your own creation.

53. Cut out two 4x3 inch pieces of muslin for the arms and two 3x3 inch pieces for the legs. The legs will need a shorter piece of muslin because half of the leg is made of clay. The width and length of the muslin are just approximate at this point. Place the forearm part of the armature on the edge of the muslin. Place the lower leg armature on the edge of the muslin. Do this for all four pieces of armature.

54. Fold the muslin over the armature.

55. Go back to the sketch and measure the arm on the figure from the top of the shoulder to the hand. It measures about 4-1/2 inches. You will need extra length for sewing and attaching the armature to the torso. A measurement

Child Arm Body Pattern

Cut 2

Child Leg Body Pattern

Cut 2

of about 5-1/4 inches will give you enough length to work with. It is better to have to shorten the pattern than to have to start over. The hip to the knee measures about 2 inches. Add an inch for the leg length. Measure the width of the muslin by leaving about 1/2 inch extra muslin for sewing the seams on the pattern.

56. Put the ruler on the wrist about 1/4 of an inch away from the clay and mark it with a dot. Draw a diagonal line from that point to the top edge of the muslin. Do the same for the leg pieces. Put the ruler on the upper leg about 1/4 of an inch away from the clay and mark with a dot. Draw a diagonal line from that point to the top edge of the muslin. The legs can stay wider because the upper leg is heavier and it will help to ensure the stability of the doll.

57. Cut the muslin arm pattern to size (see *Child Pattern for Arms and Legs*). Before sewing these pieces, put the arm and leg muslin on a piece of graph paper and trace it. Mark it and cut it out for future use.

58. With a sewing machine, stitch all four pieces leaving 1/4 inch seam allowance.

Attaching Muslin to Arm and Leg Armature

59. Attach muslin pattern to arms and legs by pulling the pieces over each of the arms and legs so that the right side of the muslin is covering the right side of the arms and legs. Pull the material down just below the ridges. Make sure the seams of the material are in the back of the legs and on the palm side of the hands.

60. Fill the ridges of the armature with glue (see *Clown— Attaching Muslin to Arm and Leg Armature #60*). Pull the muslin up over the glued ridges. Secure with a small piece of thin wire (floral wire works well).

61. Let the pieces dry. When the glue has dried, pull the muslin up to form the cloth part of the arms and legs.

Assembling the Armature

62. Using the *Child Figure Sketch* as a guide, match the leg armature to the drawing. Let the shoes fall below the last line. Twist the leg wires around the torso wire armature and secure the wire with pliers.

63. Once the legs are in place, put the doll back on the figure and put the arms where they should fall using the sketch as a guide. Twist arm wires around the top of the torso wire armature and secure them with a pliers.

Stuffing the Body

64. Wrap the armature wire with masking tape. This will soften and help pad the armature for stuffing. Stuff the arms and legs with polyester batting. Use a thin dowel stick or pencil to firmly and evenly stuff all limbs. Wrap a strip of quilt batting around the torso armature to flesh it out and aid the pattern making.

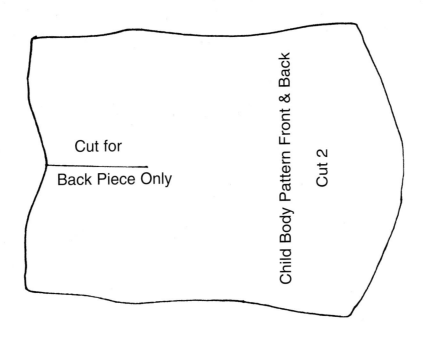

Child Body Pattern Front & Back

Cut 2

Cut for

Back Piece Only

Torso Pattern

65. Place tracing paper or wax paper over the *Child Figure Sketch* and draw the body from the top of the shoulders to just below the hips. Remove from sketch and cut it out.

66. Transfer this pattern to graph paper and add 1/4 inch on all sides for a seam allowance (see *Child Body Pattern*). Cut out the pattern and mark it. Transfer the pattern to the muslin and cut two, for the front and the back. Cut out the pattern and mark it front and back. Draw a straight line about 1-1/2 inches long down the center of this pattern, marking it "back only." This will be the opening to get the pattern over the doll's body

67. Sew the shoulder and side seams leaving 1/4 inch seam allowances. Turn the pattern to the right side and at the center of the neck edge on one pattern piece only, cut a line about 1-1/2 inches down. This will be the opening that will allow you to get the pattern over the doll.

68. Pull the muslin pattern over the doll and use the leg, arm, and neck openings to stuff the torso part of the doll. Do not over-stuff the body. Hand sew around the leg and arm openings. Sew the back and neck opening closed.

Painting Shoes

69. Using acrylic paints, paint the body of the shoe ivory. Mix a bit of brown and ivory creating a slightly darker shade for the moccasin top. Mix more brown with ivory for a darker shade for the soles of the shoes. Let dry. End with a matte finish and again let them dry.

Tights

70. Cut the foot off an old pair of opaque ivory pantyhose. Cut a 5 inch length of stocking. Cut the stocking in half length-wise.

71. Use a toothpick to apply clear drying glue between the shoe

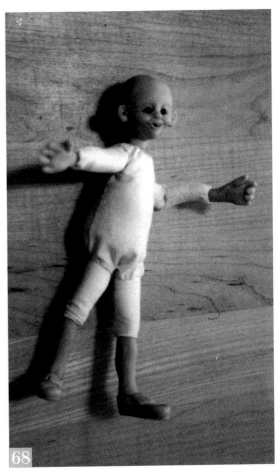

68

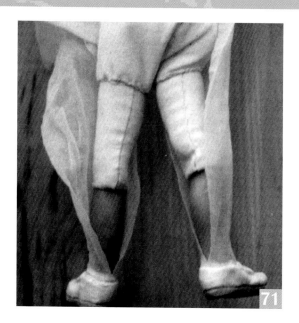

and the leg groove. Start in the back of the leg and fit the pantyhose into the grove with a toothpick, making sure the edges of the stocking do not show. When bringing the stocking around to the back, leave just enough stocking to be able to sew a seam. Trim the excess stocking and let them dry.

72. With invisible thread, sew the stocking seam, holding and folding the stocking inward as you go up the leg. Keep sewing until you reach the top of the leg. Do the same for the other leg.

73. With the thicker panty part of the hose, cut out a square about 5 inches.

74. Place the material over the front of the doll and fold the top and bottom edge under.

75. Sew around each leg, crotch, and up the back seam of doll body. Sew the hem and gather the pantyhose around the waist to make panties.

Slip

76. Cover the front of the doll with a piece of lace trimmed material. It should be double the width for both sides. Then, trim it to fit the lower portion of the doll. Leave extra material on the sides and at the waist for hemming.

77. Fold the material in half and sew up the seam which will be placed in the back. Turn down the waist. The length of the slip is measured by the point where the muslin touches the clay leg. We do not want to show that, so leave the length a little longer. Hand stitch the hem while the material is on doll with a gathered stitch and pull in the waist a little.

Blouse

78. Use the child arm and body pattern to make the blouse out of muslin (see *Child Sleeve Pattern—page 67*). Place the pattern pieces on graph paper and add 3/4 of an inch to each side of the upper blouse pattern to mea sure 4-1/2 inches. This will allow extra room for a full gathered cap sleeve. Taper the pattern down to the same wrist measurement as the body pattern.

79. Use the upper 3/4 of the body pattern for the blouse. Place the body pattern on graph paper and a with ruler, add 1/2 inch to each side of the body pattern for blouse fullness. Taper shoulders by 1/4 of an inch.

80. Mark these new pattern pieces. Draw a dotted line down the center of the new blouse pattern (see *Child Blouse Pattern—page 67*). Mark "cut down front only."

81. Cut out two front and back blouse patterns and two arm blouse patterns from muslin. Sew the sides of blouse and shoulder seams together leaving 1/4 inch seam allowance. Cut straight down the front of the blouse. This will be hand sewn later.

82. Gather 2 inches in the center of the sleeve for a cap effect and pull. Fold the sleeves in half and sew up the seams leaving 1/4 inch seam allowance.

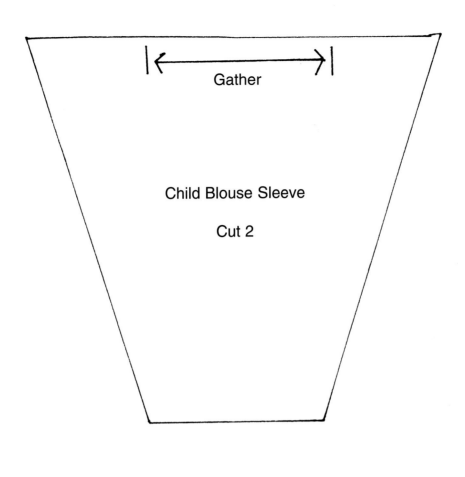

Gather

Child Blouse Sleeve

Cut 2

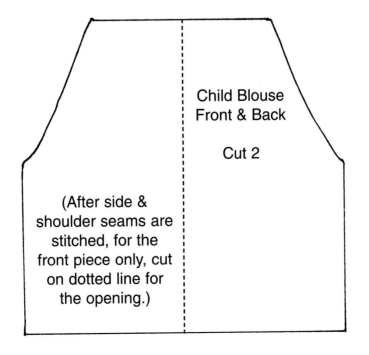

Child Blouse
Front & Back

Cut 2

(After side &
shoulder seams are
stitched, for the
front piece only, cut
on dotted line for
the opening.)

Inserting sleeves

83. The blouse is still wrong side out. Slide right side of the sewn sleeve into armhole (right sides are together) and match the seams at underarms and pin. With pins, make sure the gathered part of the sleeve material is spaced evenly at the top of the sleeve. Hand sew the sleeves to the blouse. Press with an iron.

84. Put the blouse on the doll. Fold up the excess wrist material. Fold a little bit of the material in going down the left front edge of the blouse and stitch.

85. Choose a very thin, delicate lace trim for the collar and the cuffs of the blouse. Hand sew on blouse. With a thin needle and tiny pearl beads for buttons, place and sew down the front of blouse and at the side of the cuff.

Skirt and Suspenders

86. I have chosen a piece of pleated upholstery trim for the skirt. Working with this is very easy because the pleats are already made and the material doesn't need to be hemmed. Measure around the doll and cut the trim just big enough to fold in a bit and sew up the back. (If you are using regular material, wrap the material around the doll twice in order to create a gathered skirt effect. Hem both the waist and hemline.) Place the skirt on the doll and hand sew up back seam.

87. Take two strips of material and cut them long enough to start at the front waist of the skirt, go over the shoulders, and end crossed at the back of the waist of the skirt. Leave enough material to tuck in suspenders. Make the strips wide enough so the material can be turned in on both sides and stitched. The suspenders should not be too wide as they will detract from the rest of the costume.

88. Tuck suspenders into front of skirt and tack in place with 1 or 2 stitches. Bring suspenders over the shoulders and cross in back. Tuck the edges in and tack in place with 1 or 2 stitches.

89. Hand stitch around the waist of the skirt to secure.

Fancy Socks

90. Find another thin, delicate trim which complements the costume of the doll.

91. Fill the groove between the shoe and the tights with a tooth pick and clear-drying glue. With the toothpick, start at the center back of the heel and tuck in the trim around the shoe. When you have come full-circle, tuck in the raw edges of the back seam and join by gluing. Let them dry. Fold down the top of the lace to look like socks.

Eyelashes

92. If you choose to make the eyelashes out of mohair, try to pick out the stronger individual strands. If that isn't possible, you may want to try false eyelashes purchased from a store or a doll supplier. Eyelashes purchased from a craft store or catalogue may also work. Using tweezers, pick up individual strands and cut them up for eyelashes.

93. With tweezers, dip one end in clear-drying glue and glue each individual lash to the top of the eyelids. Try to space them evenly. Let them dry. Trim with a small manicuring scissors.

Painting

94. Use a mixture of red and white to create a soft dark pink color for the lips. It should look more natural than lipstick. End with a matte finish. Mix a bit of red and a dab of brown for the inside of the mouth. Mix a bit of white with a dab of yellow for the teeth. Water down a bit of white and apply it to the upper eyelids. Mix a bit of ivory with a dab of brown and with a toothpick, make tiny dots along cheeks and bridge of nose for freckles.

95. Fingernails are neutral. Lightly apply a bit of pink and white mixed together. Let them dry and end with a matte finish.

Eyebrows

96. Use the same auburn mohair you will use for the doll wig. Cut a thin strip of hair from the mohair for the eyebrows. Use clear-drying glue and a toothpick to outline the brow line on doll.

97. With a pair of tweezers, apply bits of hair to the brow. Let them dry and trim with small manicuring scissors.

Wig

98. Using auburn mohair, divide a lengthy piece of hair about 8 inches long in half. About 1/4 down from one end, tie with matching thread. Braid these two strips leaving about the same 1/4 unbraided hair tied at other end. Tie these ends with a thin ribbon.

99. Glue wisps of hair to the sides and the back of the neck.

100. Cut two more strips of mohair about 4 inches in length. Divide in half. With a hot glue gun, glue under two strips of hair on top of the head to resemble a middle part. Cut a thin strip of hair and place it straight across the forehead of the doll for bangs. Use a hot glue gun to secure.

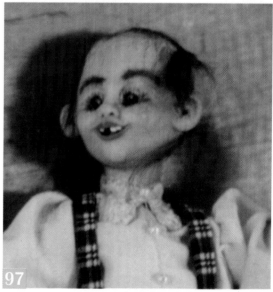

101. Turn the head to the back and with a hot glue gun, glue the braid to the neck just below the ear.

102. Bring the braids to the front of the doll. Start wrapping the two top pieces of mohair around the rest of the head. At the back of the head, fold into French twist. You may need to try this a few times before you get the look you desire. Aim the hot glue gun to the inside of the twist, and apply vertically. Work fast as hot glue dries quickly. Pinch the French twist together with fingers.

103. Make a small black bow at the back of the head out of a thin piece of black velvet or black seam binding. Use a hot glue gun to secure.

Finishing

104. Using a bit of blush on a Q-tip, apply to the cheeks, forehead, tip of the nose and the outer part of hands.

105. Put a Teddy Bear or a toy in the doll's hand. ■

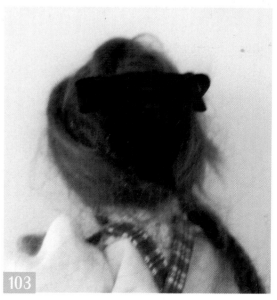

Bibliography

Bullard, Helen, *The American Doll Artist Volume I*, The Summit Press Ltd., 1965.

Faigin, Gary, *The Artist's Complete Guide to Facial Expressions*, New York: Watson-Guptill Publications, 1990.

Grubbs, *Modeling a Likeness in Clay*, New York: Watson-Guptill Publications, 1982.

Life Goes to the Movies, Time-Life Books, Inc., 1975.

Lucchesi, Bruno and Margit Malmstrom, *Modeling the Head in Clay Sculpture*, New York: Watson-Guptill Publications, 1979.

Peck, Stephen Rogers, *Atlas of Human Anatomy for the Artist*, Oxford University Press, Inc., 1951.

Racinet, Albert, *The Historical Encyclopedia of Costumes*, Facts on File, Inc., 1988.

The Best of Life, Time-Life Books, Inc., 1973.